T0339754

Branding Masculinity

Branding Masculinity examines two ideologies of masculinity—one typifying rural agricultural areas and the other found in urban, business settings. Comparisons are made between these two current forms of masculinity and both similarities and differences are identified. Six product categories compose the Constellation of Masculinity for both groups. Hirschman selects a masculine prototype brand from each category and presents a detailed analysis of the images, language and marketing actions used to create the brand's masculinity over time. Using her method, marketers for other brands will be equipped to enhance the masculine status of their brands as well.

Branding Masculinity proposes that masculine brands are *made*, not born. Masculinity is an enduring cultural ideal that can be attached to a variety of products and brands by the appropriate use of symbols, icons and images.

Scholars from various disciplines within the fields of branding, marketing, public relations and corporate identity will see this book as vital in continuing the academic discourse in the field. It will serve as a respected reference resource for researchers, academics, students and policy makers alike.

Elizabeth C. Hirschman is a Professor of Marketing at the University of Virginia's College at Wise, USA. She is the author of over 250 scholarly publications in the fields of consumer behavior, marketing, advertising, semiotics, social psychology, psychology and anthropology. She is a Past President and Fellow of the Association for Consumer Research and has been named as one of the most cited persons in the field of business and economics by the Institute for Scientific Information.

Routledge Interpretive Marketing Research
Edited by Stephen Brown, *University of Ulster, Northern Ireland*

Recent years have witnessed an 'interpretive turn' in marketing and consumer research. Methodologies from the humanities are taking their place alongside those drawn from the traditional social sciences.

Qualitative and literary modes of marketing discourse are growing in popularity. Art and aesthetics are increasingly firing the marketing imagination.

This series brings together the most innovative work in the burgeoning interpretive marketing research tradition. It ranges across the methodological spectrum from grounded theory to personal introspection, covers all aspects of the postmodern marketing 'mix,' from advertising to product development, and embraces marketing's principal subdisciplines.

Also available in Routledge Interpretive Marketing Research series:

Branding Masculinity

Tracing the Cultural Foundations of
Brand Meaning

Elizabeth C. Hirschman

Routledge
Taylor & Francis Group

NEW YORK AND LONDON

First published 2016
by Routledge
605 Third Avenue, New York, NY 10017

and by Routledge
2 Park Square, Milton Park, Abingdon, Oxon OX14 4RN

First issued in paperback 2021

Routledge is an imprint of the Taylor & Francis Group, an informa business

Publisher's Note
The publisher has gone to great lengths to ensure the quality of this
reprint but points out that some imperfections in the original copies
may be apparent.

Library of Congress Cataloging-in-Publication Data
A catalog record for this title has been requested

ISBN 13: 978-1-03-224256-9 (pbk)
ISBN 13: 978-1-138-93339-2 (hbk)

DOI: 10.4324/9781315676739

Typeset in Times New Roman
by Apex CoVantage, LLC

Perhaps the most distinctive skill of professional marketers is their ability to create, maintain, enhance and protect brands.

(Kotler and Keller 2014, p. 237)

Contents

Figures

1 Tracing Masculinity

Most of the 3,000 business books published each year are about branding. The great majority of these, as well as academic branding studies, focus their attention on one or a few brands and then work outward to examine competitive positioning, image in the minds of consumers, perceived attributes and benefits and market share trajectory (e.g., Holt and Thomson 2004). But should not brand meaning come from the marketplace itself? Is not consumer culture a brand's ultimate—and necessary—foundation (McCracken 1988)? The present book begins with a key cultural construct—masculinity—upon which several popular brands position themselves, such as Old Spice grooming products, and works forward to identify which brands actually are seen by consumers as being masculine. In the process, I outline a new procedure for creating brand meaning—one that is anchored firmly in consumer culture.

Masculinity in Cultural Context

Definitions and constructions of masculinity vary within popular culture and across the social sciences (see, e.g., Kimmel, Mean and Connell 2004). For example, Shaw and Watson (2011, p. 1) comment, "American popular culture in the new millennium exemplifies how varied, open, relative, contradictory and fluid masculinities can be." This instability in a core cultural construct can make positioning a brand as representing masculinity a difficult and ongoing task. And yet, there are cultural constancies underlying masculinity as well. For example, Connell (2005) identifies the primary structural foundation of white, heterosexual, western masculinity as *social hegemony*, which asserts male gender superiority in society. This position is maintained through male control over *dominant societal institutions*, such as the military, government and corporate organizations. White, heterosexual masculinity tends to marginalize other cultural forms of masculinity, such as those designated by race or sexual orientation (Kimmel 2012).

Kimmel (2012), like Connell (2005), also proposes that there are discernible constancies in the American cultural notion of masculinity—especially that embraced by white, middle- and working-class heterosexual males. McCullough (2008, p. 16) describes this type of man as "a husband [who] comes home every night and sweeps his wife into his arms. . . . A family [man] who is able to be trusted and depended on. . . . A wise man who is, in fact, wise . . . [Such men see a] world in which they set out each day to slay the dragons that seek to inflict hurt and pain on family and society."

These men also seem to attach their sense of self to the continuously circulating masculine stereotypes that have endured over time: GI Joe, the jock, the macho man, the knight in shining armor, action-hero man, the Marlboro Man, the cowboy, the outlaw (e.g., Holt and Thompson 2004; Mark and Pearson 2001; Reeser 2010). This is significant for marketers, because it reinforces the practicality of utilizing such iconic linkages to help create brand meaning (Mark and Pearson 2001).

The Male Body

There is general agreement within both the popular culture and social science literatures that while gender roles of masculinity (and femininity) are inculcated from an early age, the physical body (i.e., male, female) one inhabits also exerts a large influence on being masculine or being feminine (Watson and Shaw 2011). As Connell (2005, p. 45) states it,

> Mass culture generally assumes there is a fixed, true masculinity. We hear of "real men," "natural men," and the "deep masculine." . . . True masculinity is almost always thought to proceed from men's bodies . . .

Or, as Kimmel (2012, p. 238) puts it most recently,

> We're pumping up and working out obsessively to make our bodies impervious masculine machines . . . while we adorn ourselves with signifiers of a bygone era of unchallenged masculinity, donning Stetson cologne, Chaps clothing, and Timberland boots as we drive in our Cherokees and Denalis to conquer the urban jungle . . . We spend our leisure time in upscale topless bars and watching Spike TV.

But the mind is a cultural mind and the body is a cultural body. That is, these stereotypes of masculinity are shaped by culture and differ across times and cultures. They are shaped by personal experiences, media and advertising and reinforced by parents, teachers, friends and colleagues. And these same stereotypes are encoded and expressed in the products we buy, the clothes we wear, the cars we drive and the foods we eat.

The Branding of Masculinity

Social science and popular culture commentary might have remained comfortably beyond the direct interest of marketers had it not been for the sea change in the cultural expressions of masculinity that occurred during the

1990s. Several observers noted that it was in the decades of the 1990s and 2000s that masculinity became commoditized and marketed (Kimmel 2012). As women increasingly entered previously male domains of the workforce—in both blue-collar and professional occupations—as well as other traditional male strongholds such as the military and professional sports—masculinity itself became "problematized," just as it had briefly during World War II when women had also occupied "masculine" professions (Honey 1984). A man could no longer be labeled masculine merely because he performed manual labor, drove a truck, served in the armed forces, held political office, drove a police car or owned a business. Women now did these things too—although not in equal numbers or with equal authority (U.S. Department of the Census 2010).

This provided an entry point for the marketing of masculine-branded products. With the traditional occupational anchors of masculinity eroding, the opportunity was ripe for masculinity to be packaged and promoted (Holt and Thompson 2005; Kimmel 2012), just as femininity had been for a longer period of time (de Grazia 1996; Forty 1986; Kirkham 1996; Sparke 1995). Marketers advertised that one now could *purchase* masculinity in the form of their brand (Buerkle 2011). Cultural commentators agreed. Faludi (1999), for example, declared that "men are surrounded by a culture that encourages them to play almost no functional public roles, only decorative or consumer ones . . . [Manhood] is now displayed, not demonstrated" (quoted in Boudreau 2011, p. 37). However, as I shall show, the present study disputes that claim.

But what, exactly, is the cultural masculinity that brands are tying themselves to? It is not enough merely to state or claim that one's brand is masculine or to park it next to an archetypal cowboy. There must be a public perception of resonance and authenticity if the brand-masculinity linkage is to be accepted as valid. Before male consumers seeking to "drape themselves in masculinity" will accept given brands as masculine, there must be cultural evidence that the linkage is genuine. Thus, two key issues confronting marketers are (1) What aspects of contemporary culture are viewed as masculine by consumers? (2) What brands are believed to represent it?

The present book draws upon more than 300 interviews conducted with men and women across two generations—those aged 17 to 35 and those aged 40 to 60. Further, the interviews took place with persons living in two very different areas of the contemporary United States—the urban Northeast and the rural Southeast. What we learn is that *there is* a fundamental set of product categories, attitudes, activities and brands that are viewed as representing masculinity in American culture. Despite some regional and gender differences—which will be discussed in detail—there is a general cultural consistency in both the meaning and representation of masculinity. It is upon this semiotic ground that marketing efforts intended to construct a masculine positioning in the marketplace are best located.

The study introduces an inductive procedure that moves from the conceptual level to the brand level over a series of stages. By so doing, we are not only able to trace the beliefs consumers hold concerning masculinity but also to follow these beliefs through sets of activities, objects, product categories and, ultimately, brands, themselves. The result is a clarified sense of how important or unimportant specific brands are to men's sense of masculinity and the identification of the product categories in which these brands are located. The study additionally sheds light on the retail outlets deemed appropriate for locating and purchasing masculine products and brands. We learned that brands can draw masculinity from their retail surroundings and, conversely, carrying masculine brands helps create the retail ambience desired by consumers searching for masculine products.

Tracing Cultural Masculinity: Regional Realities

Because cultural conceptions of masculinity have been found by some researchers to vary across different regions of the United States (Friend 2009; Watts 2008), data were collected over a three-year period across two geographic areas: urban sections of the Northeast and rural portions of the Southeast. As will be reported, there are some regional differences in masculinity, yet despite these, there is still a bedrock constancy of masculinity, regardless of location.

An interview guide was prepared and field tested in both areas (see Exhibit 1). Potential interviewees were identified through contacts at nearby businesses and through the two universities at which I work. The interviews were conducted by the lead investigator and graduate student assistants in each area of the study. We used the *constant comparative method* advocated by Glaser (1978), Corbin and Strauss (2008) and others (see, e.g., Birks and Mills 2011; Bowen 2008; Charmaz 2006). This meant that as interviews were collected, each was read first as a unit and then compared to those already in hand. This process continued until a stable set of concepts had emerged in response to each question in each region. As initial concepts began to emerge, for example, moral characteristics such as 'courage' and 'honor,' these were then challenged using incoming interviews until a stable (i.e., saturated) set of meanings was arrived at. Conceptual structures were developed separately for the Northeast/urban and Southeast/rural regions.

Interviews were either tape recorded and transcribed or recorded in field notes by the interviewer. While all respondents were promised anonymity, few actually requested it. The respondents were white, heterosexual males and females between the ages of 17 and 35 or 40 and 60 and ranged from high school students to senior professionals. In both regions, the socioeconomic status ranged from blue collar to professional; however, the Northeast regional sample exhibited somewhat higher educational attainment and socioeconomic status, which is demographically characteristic of this region (United States Bureau of the Census 2010).

The interviews were designed to start with the *concept* of masculinity—as viewed by the participant—and then extend the discussion to the individual's father, activities and possessions until, finally, the respondent was asked to name brands he or she perceived to be masculine. By structuring the discussion in this way, we were able to generate material related to branding-as-embedded-within-masculinity rather than beginning with a brand or brands and working outward toward masculinity.

By moving from the cultural concept toward brands, we are better able to identify those brands that are deemed to represent authentic masculinity within the culture and to see in what ways they are anchored to cultural notions of masculinity. Additionally, by comparing two diverse geographic regions, we are able to obtain a much clearer picture of which brands are generally seen as masculine in American culture versus those that may represent this concept only on a regional basis. Finally, by interviewing both men and women, we are able to discern if there are gender differences in perceptions of masculinity. If gender differences are present, this may suggest that marketers should use different semiotic imagery when directing communications about masculine-positioned brands to men and to women, for example as gifts for a boyfriend or Father's Day.

The research procedure also enabled me to determine if there were shifts in what masculinity means between the present generation and that of one's father, an important piece of information for marketers who might wish to appeal to both the older and younger age cohorts in their advertising. Using this methodology, the brand-centric focus of prior marketing studies is avoided and a more accurate view of a given brand's ability to represent the cultural concept—in this case, masculinity—is achieved.

To provide an overview, let's first take a look at some of the regional differences shown in Exhibits 2 through 5. When asked to talk about "What does masculinity mean to you?," male respondents in the Northeast/urban region placed *primary* emphasis on their mental and personality traits. This is consistent with social science research indicating that male success in corporate institutions requires mental traits of decision making and rationality (see, e.g., Kimmel 2012). The activities they mentioned centered on athletics (e.g., "good at sports"), household repairs and some manual labor (e.g., "good with hands"). However, the bulk of perceived masculinity for these Northeastern urban men is seen to reside in one's mind and demeanor. Notably, *no objects* and *no brands* were mentioned as representing masculinity within the Northeastern interviewee set.

As we turn to Exhibit 3, which displays the structure of the Southeast/rural respondents' discussion, the most prominent and striking regional difference in masculinity was the content of the Activities dimension. Here we see clearly the *traditional* conception of masculine action (e.g., Twitchell 2006). Those interviewed in the Southeastern/rural region emphasized being a breadwinner/good provider and patriarchy (i.e., the subordination of women), which are traditional aspects of masculinity (Kimmel 2012). Other regional differences included a greater emphasis on being a risk taker, having courage, territoriality and individuality. This, we propose, is akin to Holt and Thompson's Rebel model (2005) and consistent with the agricultural and manual labor economy of rural areas (Friend 2009).

The activities named also varied across regions. While the Northeast and Southeast overlapped in citing *physical labor* as masculine, the Southeastern/rural respondents additionally named "eating meat," "shooting guns," "heterosexuality" and even impolite behaviors (e.g., farting) as representing masculinity. Further, the Southern men named objects—raw steaks, cold beer, cars—as representing masculinity and even named one brand, Grizzly tobacco, a chewing tobacco/dip, as being masculine. Significantly, this was the only brand named by any respondent at this level of analysis, suggesting that masculinity, the concept, is *not* anchored by brands, contrary to Faludi (1999).

Generational Differences

Masculinity, as a cultural construct, is fluid; it can shift and take on new meanings over time. I wanted to learn if the present generation of young men believed there were shifts in masculine ideology from the previous generation to their own. They did. Among the Northeastern/urban respondents (Exhibit 4), the present generation (ages 17 to 35) believed their fathers were more emotionally restricted, dominant (and domineering) and more insistent at being "the head of the house" and the "breadwinner" than they themselves are. One brand, a BMW automobile, was mentioned as representing masculinity for this older generation of men.

Southeastern/rural men in the 17- to 35-year age group saw their fathers as placing more emphasis on "keeping one's word," providing for their families and being physically strong—further evidence of patriarchy and gender dominance characterizing Southern/rural masculinity (Friend 2009). As one respondent put it, to be masculine in his father's generation was "to be a good father and husband, but not focus too much on the wife's wants."

The contrasting prior generational masculinities of these two regions are brought into clearer contrast by the two extended quotes that follow:

> *From what I recall, my father would most likely define his masculinity by how many girlfriends he could maintain at one time, or what kind of BMW he drove. But most importantly, it was not what his family thought of him, but more so what his peers thought.*
>
> (Michael, age 33, Northeast/urban)

> *He was a football player in high school and began working in the coal mines when he was 17 years old. He's close to 50 now and still works in those mines. My father is the hardest of workers; he worked hurt, sick, and tired . . . He instilled a sense of accountability in me. He emphasized being truthful . . . Winning was huge to him, almost as much as being tough . . . He taught me that crying. . .would emasculate me . . . I would be less of a man.*
>
> (Robert, age 24, Southeast/rural)

The form of masculinity we found in the Northeast, even in the prior generation, seems to express a greater orientation toward the public display of success, while that in the Southeast is grounded more deeply in stoicism and self-denial.

Masculine Activities

Exhibits 6 and 7 depict the set of activities perceived as masculine in each region. Both groups of men saw "hanging out" (often at bars) with male friends as masculine activities; Kimmel (2012) terms this homo-sociality and views it as a cornerstone of American masculinity. Both groups also mention "pursuing women" as a masculine activity; this is also often mentioned as a characteristic of American masculinity (Kimmel 2012). Participating in contact sports such as football, hockey, soccer, boxing/fighting/martial arts, weightlifting/working out are seen as masculine by men in both groups. Notably, these all require aggressiveness as well as athletic ability.

There were some subtle but telling regional differences. For example, the Northeast/urban men see *watching* sports as masculine and engaging in "intellectual gaming," such as fantasy football, as masculine, whereas these were not mentioned by men in the Southeastern/rural region. In contrast, men in the rural South name car racing, bowling, wrestling and four-wheeling as masculine pursuits. From a branding perspective, these regional variations in masculinity are likely to be significant. Men in the Southeast seem to view physically demanding *participation* as more indicative of masculinity, whereas men in the Northeast more value *knowledge* about sporting activities. The "rugged" orientation of Southeastern rural masculinity is also reflected in the many mentions of *hunting* as a masculine pursuit (an activity not named in any of the Northeastern interviews). Southern men also appeared to more highly value mechanical/automotive/construction projects as indicators of masculinity.

Two important regional occupational differences are present. First, men in the Southeast/rural area named criminal justice/police work and serving in the military as signifiers of masculinity, whereas those in the Northeast/urban area did not. Notably, the Southeast is markedly higher in military enlistments as a percentage of the population than is the Northeast (Watts 2008). Second, "dipping"—using chewing tobacco products—was mentioned by several respondents as a masculine activity. Tobacco usage rates are higher in the Southeast than the Northeast, the region being the source of most US–grown tobacco (Watts 2008), and it is interesting to note that chewing tobacco use (as opposed to smoking cigarettes) is seen as uniquely masculine there.

These regional overlaps and variations suggest that branding efforts may need to be modulated regionally depending upon the product category. Also important is the fact that *no specific brands* were mentioned as signifiers of masculinity by either regional group in the context of activities.

Masculine Products

When men were asked to discuss "products you think of as masculine," the results yielded several brand names, some of which were common to both regions, while others were unique to one region. This is managerially important because, ideally, a national brand seeking to position itself as "masculine" would want this image to be present across all areas of the country. Further, regional masculine brands also should be of interest to marketers because they likely are linked to key *behaviors or attitudes indigenous to the area*. Marketers seeking to enter such a regional market could benefit from researching these brands and gaining an understanding of their appeal.

There were some significant regional differences in the *product categories* deemed to be masculine. For example, while both groups of men named "beer" as masculine (and, indeed, virtually all beer advertising targets men), Southeastern men also named "dip" (chewing tobacco) as masculine, indicating that *both* product categories are seen as ways to display one's manliness.

Vehicles viewed as masculine also varied by region. The Northeastern/urban men saw "cars," especially sports cars and SUVs, as representing masculinity; Jeeps, Corvettes and Mustangs were frequently mentioned. But the Southeastern/rural men preferred pickup trucks, naming the Chevy Tahoe, specifically, and also the Mustang sports car.

Both groups see consumer electronics as being masculine; for example, the Xbox is cited in both regions. However, the Southeastern/rural respondents named a greater variety of electronics, ranging from laptop computers to GPS equipment. It is possible that this group's *general mechanical orientation* may play a larger role in their masculinity and that they are more attuned to electronic gadgetry (Friend 2009; Hirschman, Brown and Maclaran 2006).

For both groups, *Old Spice* deodorant was spontaneously mentioned as a masculine grooming product, indicating that the *Old Spice* marketing communications campaign, "Smell like a man, man," has been successful in creating a cross-regional masculine positioning. Tim McGraw cologne was named by an interviewee in the Northeast as representing masculinity. McGraw is a country-western singer from the Southeastern region who typically wears cowboy apparel when performing. The cowboy, of course, is one of the "circulating icons of cultural masculinity" (Cawelti 1984) mentioned earlier. In Chapter Two, I will argue that the Southeastern regional culture serves as the semiotic foundation for American masculinity but that the Northeastern region has contributed an important archetypal figure to the masculine pantheon.

The most powerful demarcation between the two regions was the very large emphasis placed on *weapons*—especially guns—by men in the Southeastern/rural region. As can be seen in Exhibits 8 and 9, Southeastern men "skewed" toward hunting activities not only in mentioning rifles and shotguns but also by describing "coon stretchers" and "defleshers," both instruments used to field dress animals, as masculine tools. They are also more oriented toward outdoor and wilderness pursuits, which is logical given their rural environment (and see also Watts 2008).

Masculine Brands

Toward the end of each interview, men and women were asked what *brands* they thought of as masculine. This was the first point at which the interviewer explicitly used the term 'brand,' although as we have seen in earlier discussion, some persons spontaneously brought specific brand names into the conversation. What is compelling about the responses to this query is not only the brand names mentioned but also the *product categories* into which they fall. Across both regions, brands in the categories of *weapons, vehicles, tools, media/technology, grooming, apparel, alcohol* and *tobacco* were named. In essence, these product categories form the marketplace sources for the purchase and display of one's masculinity. Each category, and its *brand anchors*, are discussed in what follows.

Weapons

Weapons, especially guns and rifles, have long been considered a masculine arena of consumption (e.g., Souter 2012). Notably, men in both the Northeast/ urban and Southeast/rural regions named *Smith & Wesson* as a brand of gun representing masculinity. This is likely linked to the several *Dirty Harry* motion pictures starring Clint Eastwood that popularized the Smith & Wesson hand-gun (see Souter 2012). A comparison of Exhibits 10 and 11 shows that several additional gun brands were mentioned by men in the Southeast as masculine, such as *Beretta* and *Winchester*, suggesting that firearms play a larger role in defining masculinity in this region.

Vehicles

Perhaps no motor vehicle is more strongly associated with masculinity in the United States than the *Harley-Davidson* brand of motorcycles (Schouten and McAlexander 1995). Notably, although none of the respondents *actually owned* a motorcycle, several cited this brand as representing masculinity. A mountain bike brand, *Trek*, was mentioned in the Northeastern/urban sample. However, among Southeastern men, the pickup truck, especially *Ford* and *Dodge* brands, and "muscle" cars, for example, *Mustang* and *Camaro*, are more commonly mentioned.

Tools and Equipment

The Sears brand of *Craftsman* tools is named as representing masculinity by both regional groups of men. This suggests that Sears has been effective in anchoring this brand in American men's cultural conceptions of manliness. Similarly, *John Deere* is also prominent as a perceived masculine brand among both groups. Possessing these brands is believed to 'signal' one's masculinity to both the self and others (Belk 1988).

Apparel

Among the apparel brands named spontaneously during the interviews, only *Nike* was present in both the Northeastern/urban and Southeastern/rural regional cultures. This is a strong testimony to Nike's advertising and other marketing efforts. Even though it has also aggressively targeted women, Nike has succeeded in becoming an *anchor brand* for the concept of masculinity. Notably, specific apparel brands seem to hold a larger place in the consciousness of Southeastern/rural men as signifying masculinity. Only four apparel brands were named in the Northeastern sample, while the Southeastern sample named sixteen discrete brands. Apparently, in the southeastern United States, clothing really does "make the man."

Grooming Products

Three brands of men's deodorant—*Old Spice*, *Axe* and (Gillette) *Speed Stick*—are named by men in both regions. The current Old Spice advertising theme of "Smell like a man, man" was even cited by some. What is notable about this is that these three brands, though promoting what could be considered a *convenience* product, have succeeded in positioning themselves as anchoring points for the American cultural conception of masculinity. This suggests that marketing *does have potency* in shaping social belief systems, having succeeded in making a descenting grooming product an indicator of masculinity. There was a time when smelling natural or sweaty would have been perceived as masculine, and for one gender, it still does. I explore this phenomenon in Chapter Three, where we learn that *women* still associate sweat with masculinity in men.

Alcohol and Tobacco

Masculinity has long been associated with the consumption of liquor and beer (Kimmel 2012) as well as tobacco (Kimmel 2012) in the United States. Among the men to whom we spoke, however, only the *Budweiser* brand is seen as a consistent symbol of masculinity. Northeastern/urban men also consider *Marlboro* to be a 'manly' brand of tobacco, whereas in the Southeast, *Copenhagen* tobacco—a chewing tobacco brand—is named. There is clearly a strong, pervasive linkage in the Southeast between 'being a man' and using chewing tobacco products; one that is likely cause for public health concern. Notably the Southeastern/rural sample also viewed two soft drinks as signifying masculinity: *Gatorade* and *Mountain Dew*. Although Holt and Thomson (2005) notes the success of Pepsi in representing Mountain Dew as a national youth culture beverage, in the Southeastern region (its place of origin), the brand remains masculine.

Media, Technology and Athletics

Professional sports teams, such as the National Hockey League, are named as masculine brands by men in the Northeastern/urban sample but not by those in the Southeast/rural region. This is significant, because it suggests men in the Southeast may be less attuned to organized, professional spectacles of athletic masculinity and more oriented toward localized, on-the-ground athletic events. Supporting this thesis is the *absence* of mentions of NASCAR by the Southern men, despite the fact that the Southeast is the origin point for stock car racing (Hirschman, Brown and Maclaran 2006), and men in this region display a strong affinity with motor vehicles, as already noted. Male-oriented television channels, such as ESPN and Spike TV, were named by both groups of men. These channels seem to act as something akin to electronic 'man caves' or man havens for those we interviewed; by tuning in, one could enter a safely masculine environment.

Masculinity: The Brand Constellation

By initiating this research as an investigation of masculinity as a concept rather than branding *per se*, we are able to gain a stronger, foundational understanding of the brands Americans—at least in the Northeast and Southeast regions— associate with masculinity. By working from a core cultural concept *toward* brands that represent the concept in consumers' perceptions, we gain access to the larger semiotic structures in which brands are embedded.

The balance of this book will first explore men's and women's archetypal construals of masculinity. In Chapter Two, I will argue that men serve as conduits between the natural world and the civilized world; that masculinity is best understood as embodying the oppositional categories of human and beast. Masculine men, I propose, are those who can transport materials from the chaos, danger and threat of the wilderness and transform them into useful and valued objects of the civilized world. Concurrently, they are capable of transporting dangerous or depleted materials from the civilized world back to the natural world—or at least effecting their containment in suitable 'storage facilities,' such as prisons and garbage dumps.

In Chapter Three, I will present a deeper examination of women's conceptualizations of masculinity. I will argue that contemporary women view as masculine those men who are sexually potent, capable of beastliness in protecting them from harm and entrepreneurial in personality.

Chapters Four through Nine will examine the history of anchor brands in each of the product categories found to represent masculinity. I will present narratives for a representative brand in each category drawn from popular culture and advertising and identify the verbal and visual imagery used to create the cultural sense of its masculinity.

Exhibit 1 Interview Guide

1. What does masculinity mean to you?
2. What do you think masculinity means to your father?
3. What activities do you engage in that you think of as masculine?
4. What products do you think of as masculine?
5. What brands do you think of as masculine?

Exhibit 2 What Does Masculinity Mean to You?
Northeast Urban

Body	*Action*	*Mind*	*Objects*
• Physical strength	• Good at sports	• Personality	
• Having a penis	• Working on cars	• Logical courage	
	• Good with hands	• Tough in any situation	
	• Take care of household repairs	• Mental strength	
		• Others look up to	
	• Good fighter	• Dominant in roles	
	• Role model for children and wife	• Rational decision making	
		• Emotionally strong	
		• Authoritative power Fair and rational	
		• Know when to use force	
		• Take responsibility	

Exhibit 3 What Does Masculinity Mean To You?
Southeast Rural

Body	Action	Mind	Objects
• Physical strength • Strong body • Rough and tough	• Eating meat • Shooting guns • Complete any task • Work hard, hard labor • Being successful and powerful • Keeping job • Protecting others, family • Sexuality with women • Getting hands dirty • Farting and belching • Working out • Good father • Family provider • Others can depend on • Put food on the table and pay bills • Leader • Dominant with women • Dominant at home—wears the pants	• Intelligent • Flexibility • Knowledge • Mental strength • Loyalty • Independence • Own goals • Achievements • Honesty • Owns up to mistakes • Morality • Humor • Self-worth • Selfhood • Uniqueness and individuality • Never backs down • Boldness • Risk taker • Courage, bravery, competitive • Control fear • Control emotions • Decisive • Control self • Control situations	• Raw steaks • Cold beer • Cars • Grizzly tobacco

Exhibit 4
What Does Masculinity Mean to Your Father?
Northeast/Urban

Body	Action	Mind	Objects
	• Provide for the family • Good at job • Successful • Able to build things • Outdoorsy • All-around handy • "Bark the loudest" • Man of the house • Being a good role model • Joined armed services • Multiple girlfriends at the same time • Never ask for help • Take care of your own	• What other men think of him > family • Not show emotions • Never show weakness • Be most intimidating • Always getting your way • Decision maker • Leader of the household • Responsible	• BMW

Exhibit 5 What Does Masculinity Mean to Your Father?
Southeast Rural

Body	Action	Mind	Objects
• Physical health • Physical body • Mechanical	• Provide for the family • Care for those at home • Hardworking, keeping job • Protect family • "Higher standard than me" • "More being rough and tough" • Chasing women • Always able to dominate women • Good father and husband, but not focus on wife's wants • Protect his own	• No emotions • Intelligence • Mental strength • Keep promises • Keep one's word • Learning life lessons • Stability • Loyal • Never saying you can't • Do something • Risk taker • Honesty • Discipline • Sensible • More powerful emotions	

Exhibit 6 What Activities Are Most Masculine?
Southeast/Rural

Around the House	*Out of the House*
Hands-on work	Going to the bar
Carpentry, construction	Partying, drinking
Car repair, mechanical	Dipping tobacco
House repair, lawn care	Chasing girls, sex
Growing a beard	Talking politics
Wilderness and Outdoor Activities	*Participatory Sports*
Hunting, fishing, being outdoors	Golfing, car racing
Camping, hiking, canoeing	Soccer, hockey, fighting
Rock climbing	"Blood and guts" sports—football, wrestling four-wheeling
	Baseball, lifting, bowling
	"Throwing Stuff"
Occupations	
Criminal justice	
Army, military	

Exhibit 7 What Activities Are Most Masculine?
Northeast/Urban

Around the House	*Out of the House*
Lawn care, grilling	Hanging out with guy friends
House repair	Talking to girls, sex
Building things	
Hanging Christmas lights	
Working on cars	
Being a dad	
Make sure bills are paid	
Providing for family	
Wilderness and Outdoor Activities	*Observational Activities*
Fishing, hiking, camping	Watching sports, fantasy football

Participating in Sports	
Working out	Golfing
Hockey	Fighting
Football	Boxing
Soccer	Mixed martial arts
Hockey	Skiing
Bicycling	

Exhibit 8 Do You Own Any Products You Think of as Masculine?
Northeast/Urban

Vehicles	Electronics
SUV	46-inch TV
Jeep	Xbox Slim
Motorcycle	PlayStation
Corvette engine	
Sports car	
Mustang GTO	
Apparel	**Grooming Supplies**
Work boots	Deodorant
Sports jerseys	Soap
Jock strap	Razor
	Old Spice
	Tim McGraw cologne
Tools	**Athletic Equipment**
Jumper cables	Boxing gloves
Tools	Judo gear
Garbage can	Punching bag
Humane rat trap	Baseball and golf equipment
Miter saw	Bicycle
	Skateboards

Exhibit 9 Do You Own Any Products You Think of as Masculine?
Southeast/Rural

Vehicles	Weapons
Truck	Firearms
Muscle car	Shotgun
Chevy Tahoe truck	Knives
Mustang car	Rifle
	Sword
Electronics	**Tools**
GPS	Toolbox
Laptop, phone	Lawn mower
Xbox	Coon stretcher
Razor phone	Deflesher
iPod	

Apparel	Athletic Equipment
Socks	Exercise equipment
Ties	Weights
Suit	Punching bag
Jacket	Football
Hats	Boxing gloves
Work boots	Mountain bike
Briefcase	Fishing equipment
Sneakers	Hunting gear
Dress shoes	Outdoor equipment
Food	**Grooming Supplies**
Beer	Beard trimmer
Dip/tobacco	Deodorant
Budweiser	Razor
Old Spice	Shampoo
Axe deodorant	Speed Stick

Exhibit 10 Brands You Think Are Masculine
Northeast/Urban

Weapons	Alcohol & Tobacco
Smith & Wesson	Marlboro
	Johnny Walker
	Miller beer
	Budweiser beer
Vehicles	**Sports Teams**
Harley-Davidson	NFL
Trek bikes	NBA
	UFC
	NHL
	baseball
Tools/Equipment	**Media**
Craftsman tools	Spike TV
Snap-on tools	H-D
John Deere	NET
Grooming Products	**Apparel**
Old Spice deodorant	Calvin Klein
Axe deodorant	Wilson
Speed stick deodorant	Redwing boots
Norelco razors	Nike

Exhibit 11 Brands You Think Are Masculine

Southeast/Rural

Weapons	**Alcohol & Tobacco**
Smith & Wesson	Jack Daniel's
Beretta	Guinness
Remington	Passport scotch
Winchester	Bud Light
	Coors Light
	Yuengling
	Copenhagen tobacco
Vehicles	**Soft Drinks**
Harley-Davidson	Gatorade
Michelin tires	Mountain Dew
Trucks	
Ford	
Dodge	
Mustang	
Camaro	
Tools/Equipment	**Apparel**
Stihl	Quicksilver
Black & Decker	Everlast
John Deere	Rockport
Craftsman tools	Army Surplus
	A&F
	Polo/RL
	Express Man
	Russell Athletic
	Dick's Sporting Goods
	Nike
	Levi's
	Under Armour
	Eddie Bauer
	Men's Warehouse
	Dockers
Grooming Products	**Media**
Speed Stick	ESPN
Old Spice	Rap and metal music
Gillette razors	Xbox
Axe deodorant	
Viagra	
Brut	
Trojans	

2   Men's Perceptions of Masculinity

We begin this chapter with a sampling of the responses obtained to the first question asked: *What does masculinity mean to you?*

> *I think it is someone who is able to take on responsibilities, not shy away from adverse conditions. It's a combination . . . where you kind of picture a lumberjack, but in today's society he also wears a suit, has a good job, takes care of the family, mows the lawn, helps his wife, takes care of the kids . . . In essence it's more just about taking charge, being a strong individual, mentally, physically, emotionally, in every way. You need to be a complete person.*
>
> (Male, age 26, Northeast, married)

> *It means macho. It means to be a man. To be the head, to be the leader. To take charge. To do things right the first time. To get things done. To produce children. Like for instance a lion . . .*
>   *It's set by the genders that God or nature created.*
>
> (Male, age 56, Northeast, married with children)

> *Masculinity to me is carrying out the role that God intended for me. It is to protect and provide for my family, to be strong; to make the decisions I need to make, even in the face of tremendous difficulties. It means standing up for those who need to be defended and being willing to give my life for it. I would put my life on the line . . . to provide freedom for a girl to go to school in the Middle East or for an African to be able to eat.*
>
> (Male, age 34, Southeast, Marine)

> *One gets to see the display of masculinity in sports . . . The idea of masculinity is epitomized by the fighting spirit of these athletes, especially while injured. I can recall Brett Favre's historic NFC championship game*

against the Saints. I just couldn't believe how he was able to stand up and play each time after every vicious body-wrecking blow and hit. He never gave up! He wanted to win at any cost!

(Male, age 32, Northeast, married)

Having a hard body. I am addicted to sports . . . I was captain of the football, basketball and baseball teams in high school . . . To look and feel strong. To be able to command attention as I enter the room. I want people to look at me and see power.

(Male, age 26, Southeast, married, 2 children)

How much of a man you are. Someone who plays a sport. Being gross with dude friends. Open about farting in front of guys. Always think of someone with big beard, hairy chest . . . no pampering yourself.

(Male, age 17, Southeast, single)

Voicing my ideas and not being subservient to 'the man'; able to go my own way against the crowd. Being able to make my wife feel secure. Having the ability to take charge. Partying with guy friends and not getting arrested. Doing the messy chores, car repair, home repair, carrying bags for my wife, grilling.

(Male, age 43, Southeast, married)

As the excerpts indicate, there is a range of opinion about what masculinity means, yet as stated at the outset of the book, there is a core of meaning that remains consistent. There is also a general consensus about what masculine men *are not*: Masculine men are not physically weak, they are not cowardly, they do not become unsure of themselves, give in to pressure, run away from a fight, whine or make excuses for failure. One man I interviewed, for example, compared LeBron James with Michael Jordan, stating that Jordan was 'more masculine' than LeBron, because LeBron, though a huge, powerful, talented athlete, "whines all the time about bad refs' calls; that's not manly. Jordan just sucked it up and kept on playing." Thus, at its core of cores, masculinity is perhaps more about *attitude* than sheer size and strength.

Seven themes are present in the set of men's interviews that permit us to peer more deeply into the semiotic structure of masculinity in America. These themes are (1) the origins of masculinity in genetics and/or society; (2) masculinity encompassing both the physical body and the moral, mental and emotional aspects of a man; (3) the traditional notion of masculinity as brutish versus more recent concepts of financial success and professionalism; (4) the anchoring of masculinity in tool use, physical strength and mechanical competence versus the mind-as-machine metaphor now gaining influence in contemporary culture; (5) masculine sexuality as predatory, aggressive and fertile; masculine men are potent and can impregnate women, especially with sons; and (6) the transition from Young Rebel to Stalwart Breadwinner over the life cycle. Young single men are expected to be sexually and physically aggressive. They engage in rule breaking, adventure seeking and treasure hunting. Married men are expected to be providers and protectors for their families. (7) The capstone concept, I will argue, is that masculinity serves as a transformative status between nature and culture, wilderness and civilization, chaos and order. Masculine men serve as boundary spanners, able to function successfully in both these conceptual realms. Masculine men are responsible for removing danger, disease and evil from society and containing it in societally approved areas (e.g., toxic waste dumps, garbage dumps, prisons) while concurrently being able to transport valuable and useful materials from the natural world into society.

(1)   The Origins of Masculinity: Nature and/or Nurture

The men and women interviewed for this research expressed a continuum of opinions regarding the origins of masculinity. Though not asked directly, several volunteered opinions that masculinity was something a man was 'born with'; that is, men, *by their nature*, exhibit traits of leadership, aggressiveness, emotional control, athletic and mechanical ability, venturesomeness, a proclivity for violence, competitiveness and sexual dominance. Some interviewees saw these traits as innate, appropriate and immutable. Others in the set of respondents believed that "there is about a 50/50 split between being born with [masculinity] and learning it" as one respondent put it. And a few, very much in the minority, believed that masculinity was completely mutable, according to prevailing social trends.

Most of those to whom we talked felt that traditional masculinity was being altered but not erased by the movement of women into the workforce and other social positions formerly occupied only by men. As one married man in his thirties put it, "In my father's generation, he was the provider and the protector of the family. My wife and I both work, so I am not the only provider, but I am still the main protector." Several men in the younger generation believed that they and others in their age group are more *androgynous* than prior generations of men. They are willing and able to look after children; but they are still expected (by themselves and by the women in their lives) to do "manly chores like taking out the garbage, cleaning up dog poop, fixing things around the house and mowing the lawn."

Notably, one of the most consistent expressions was that the male interviewee's *father* served as his primary role model for masculinity—especially in terms of *attitude and morality*. Fathers who acted responsibly, "took care of things" and "provided for the family" were seen as the most admirable in modeling masculinity for their sons. Notably, none of those interviewed talked positively about fathers who had "left home" or been unable to earn a "good living."

Figure 2.1 Illustrations of Adam and Eve in the Garden of Eden. This image by Albert Dürer depicts Adam and Eve in the Garden of Eden. Adam is shown holding a written document of man's dominion over nature, while Eve is depicted being tempted by the serpent.

Source: Dürer, Albrecht. *Adam and Eve.* 1504. The Morgan Library and Museum, New York. *Wikimedia Commons.* Web. 25 Aug. 2015.

https://commons.wikimedia.org/wiki/File:Albrecht_D%C3%BCrer,_Adam_and_Eve,_1504,_Engraving.jpg

Figure 2.2 Painting of Daniel Boone crossing the Cumberland Gap. This iconic painting of Daniel Boone and his family on the Wilderness Road leading into Kentucky
through the Cumberland Gap presents Boone dressed in deerskin apparel, carrying a
long rifle and accompanied by a hunting dog. These images serve as a touchstone for
American notions of masculinity.

Source: Bingham, George Caleb. *Daniel Boone escorting settlers through the Cumberland Gap.*
1851–1852. Mildred Lane Kemper Art Museum, Missouri. *Wikimedia Commons.* Web. 25 Aug.
2015.

https://commons.wikimedia.org/wiki/File:George_Caleb_Bingham_-_Daniel_Boone_escorting_
settlers_through_the_Cumberland_Gap.jpg

(2) Masculinity Encompasses Not Only the Physical Body but Also the Moral, Mental and Emotional Aspects of a Man

Among those to whom we spoke, there is great consistency in the belief that
masculine men are large, strong and muscular. They are described as being
"in shape" and "well built" and having "great bodies." Perhaps the most commonly cited image was that of "a lumberjack in a plaid flannel shirt with a
full beard, hairy chest and an axe chopping down trees." Skinny, short, out-
of-shape, nonmuscular men were not seen as masculine. Nor were men who
were narcissistic, shaved their bodies, went to tanning salons or wore "too-tight
clothes." Gay men were described by many as being nonmasculine. Any one
having "feminine tendencies" was considered not masculine. In several of the
interviews, masculinity was described as the "opposite pole of femaleness."

Figure 2.3 Illustration of a Charles Atlas print advertisement from the 1950s. This advertisement from the 1950s encourages men to renew their manliness by creating a muscular body. Note the emphasis on upper-body development and broad shoulders. According to Buss (1994), these are indicators of masculinity attractive to women.

Source: Weird Tales. *Charles Atlas advert WeirdTalesv36n1*. 1941. *Wikimedia Commons*. Web. 25 Aug. 2015.

https://commons.wikimedia.org/wiki/File:Charles_Atlas_advert_WeirdTalesv36n1.jpg

And yet, masculinity extends beyond physical appearance. Men are said to be masculine if they are willing to sacrifice their own wants/needs for their families, to be stoic and self-denying. Men are considered masculine if they do not show fear or moral weakness; they "stand up for what is right" even if that means negative consequences.

Masculine men are said to be able to "take charge in a crisis," "do the right thing" and "take care of others" according to those to whom we spoke. In particular, masculine men were said to "never run away" from a fight, challenge or crisis. My sense is that while physical size and power are closely associated with masculinity, the core trait is *moral courage*. Cowardice is seen as the key oppositional characteristic of masculinity: better to be a courageous mouse than a cowardly lion.

(3) The Beastly Barbarian and/or the Professional Knight

There are two competing images of masculinity in the descriptions provided by those we interviewed. Almost universally, those to whom we spoke saw an important aspect of masculinity in terms of roughness, toughness and "being bad-ass." Masculine men are said to be able to consume large quantities of liquor, survive alone in the wild, "live off the land" and win bar fights. They can kill and skin animals. They are dirty, hairy and smelly—and enjoy being that way. Some described them as being "like cavemen" or "Neanderthals." Their manners are crude; clothes are unkempt, and they fart, belch and urinate in public. In short, they exhibit bestial qualities; they seem less evolved and closer to a natural state.

However, many younger men and some women see masculinity in different terms. To them, masculinity is linked to being able to finesse complex business deals, to come out "on top" in negotiations, to be able to walk into a business or social gathering and command attention. Often mixed with these descriptions is a belief that the masculine man would have very well-tailored apparel, a handsome face and articulate speech that enables him to dominate others in a face-to-face discussion. This would seem to be the legacy of contemporary culture's emphasis on *business* as the primary domain of male competition and conquest. However, several persons noted that it is not money *per se* that makes a man masculine; rather, it is success in *competing with other smart, aggressive men for money* that makes the man masculine. Wealth is depicted as the prize for winning the game, not as the primary goal in and of itself.

The central notion here seems to be one of transferring the male "field of battle" from a muddy, bloody war zone to entrepreneurial endeavor. A masculine man is one who can break the rules, outsmart his opponents and "get the deal." These battles require a different skill set than those fought in hand-to-hand combat. However, across all those interviewed, there was still a lingering acknowledgment that "when the shit hits the fan," a masculine man has to be capable of "taking out the bad guys," as one person put it.

The motion picture *Taken*, in which a divorced father who is a former Special Forces operative, played by Liam Neeson, rescues his daughter from an international prostitution ring, illustrates this concept well. In the film, the teenage daughter is kidnapped on a trip to Europe. Her stepfather, a very wealthy businessman, is unable to rescue her. However, her former SEAL father springs into action and singlehandedly gets her back before her virginity is lost to the rich Arab oil sheik who purchased her. (This film hits almost every vigilante, true-blue, red-blooded American male semiotic key that can be struck.)

(4)   Tools, Machines, Bodies, Minds

Virtually everyone to whom we spoke identified masculinity with competence at using tools and operating machines. The types of activities associated with masculinity are heavily weighted toward building things, moving things, tearing down things, repairing things and driving things. Masculine men are expected to be able to change tires, chop down trees, fight fires, shoot intruders, drive fast cars, drive large trucks, use power tools, install plumbing, hunt and kill large animals, build houses, dig through rock and repair engines. In so doing, they may need to use knives, guns, axes, screwdrivers, wrenches, air compressors and welding torches.

Men who do not have competence with at least some of these tools and machines are not deemed to be masculine. One female respondent reported that she is "disappointed" that so many men in the urban Northeast region "do not even know how to change their own tires; they always have to call the service station." On follow-up questioning, this same respondent expressed the belief that a man's not being able to change a tire might suggest deeper masculinity issues, such as an inability to fight or "be good in bed." Thus, a lack of competence in tool use/mechanical skill seems to spill over into doubts about other areas of male performance.

Male dominance of weaponry, mechanics and technology has been noted by many researchers. But perhaps less recognized is that many men view masculinity as part of a *body-as-machine* metaphor and project this view onto themselves and others. Recall the earlier excerpt about the performance of NFL quarterback Brett Favre who "kept getting back up," despite damaging blows from oncoming tacklers. Favre was able to will his machine-body to keep performing its task despite being in a 'wrecked' state. The willingness (and ability) to drive body parts past their normal limits is seen as indicating masculinity. Mythic men such as Hercules, Samson, Robert Redford's injured baseball player in *The Natural* and modern athletes such as Favre are deemed to *embody* masculinity, because they use their physical selves as machines to accomplish extraordinary feats, especially when those feats serve a moral purpose.

A recent fictional example of this would be the character played by Russell Crowe in *The Gladiator*, who managed to kill the corrupt emperor of Rome in one-on-one combat although mortally wounded himself. In such cases the semiotics are doubly powerful, because the self-sacrificing male not only over-comes virtually impossible physical challenges but also brings about a just outcome with his death.

A second fictional example of this is the role played by Arnold Schwar-zenegger in the film *Terminator II*. In the story, a hypermasculine robotic warrior takes on human qualities of morality and protectiveness toward chil-dren and women. To save a human mother and her son, who are central to the salvation of the world, the robot-warrior first destroys another machine that has been sent to slay them and then kills himself to prevent the technol-ogy he contains from being used for evil purposes. Recall the quote from the Marine from the Southeastern rural region of the United States at the beginning of this chapter who stated he would give up his own life to bring education to girls in the Middle East or food to children in Africa. Such men have extended their masculine roles as father-protectors to children other than their own.

But masculinity today also implies the ability to be dominant in the use of digital technology. The men we interviewed emphasized the importance of knowing how to operate gadgets from GPS to smartphones to online games and additionally being able to reprogram some of these devices to 'do tricks' other men's equipment could not perform. Size also matters, with the man having the largest and most intelligent digital television being seen as most masculine. Digital technology has become another area of competition, with the most cus-tomized and complex machines being the most admired.

(5)   Masculine Sexuality

This aspect of masculinity is complex yet little discussed in the social science research thus far. The prevailing sentiment among those we interviewed, both men and women, is that masculine men are sexually potent, active and aggres-sive. Younger men often stated that a masculine man is one who "pursues women," "goes to bed with a lot of women" and "likes sex." There is a definite heterosexual slant to the reports. Several persons spontaneously said that a homosexual man could *not* be masculine. This attitude is strongest among the older generation of men. When they are at a bar or "hanging out," masculine men are described as discussing having sex with women and how many women they have "scored with."

Gay men, because they are not engaged in 'scoring' with women, are there-fore viewed as not only noncompetitive but also noncompetent.

The older generation associated masculine sexuality with being able to father children, especially sons. Having multiple sons is seen as a signal of manhood and is also seen as a way for the man to leave behind a legacy. An important task, according to those we spoke with, is for the man to teach his son(s) the les-sons of manhood, how the son should conduct himself, what his values should be. A man who is unable to father sons is 'diminished' in his masculinity by his inability to leave behind this legacy. It signals a failure in his life.

Figure 2.4 Photograph of actor Channing Tatum. Channing Tatum began his working career as a male stripper and then appeared in a series of teen-audience dance movies that brought attention to his remarkably fit masculine body and athletic movements. This talent reached new heights in the semi-autobiographical film *Magic Mike*.

Source: Wcfirm. *Channing-Tatum-Unwrapped-Fighting-Press-Junket-04–2009*. 2009. *Wikimedia Commons*. Web. 25 Aug. 2015.

https://commons.wikimedia.org/wiki/File:Channing-Tatum-Unwrapped-Fighting-Press-Junket-04–2009.jpg

Figure 2.5 Photograph of actor Pierce Brosnan. Pierce Brosnan represents a masculine icon of the previous generation for his portrayal of James Bond in several motion pictures.

Source: s_burkley. *Pierce Brosnan*. Digital Image. Shutterstock. 09 Nov. 2006. Web. 03 Sept. 2015.

We will discuss women's views of masculine sexuality in more detail in Chapter Three, but a key element in their perceptions is that the man be handsome, virile and very capable sexually.

Most reported that masculine men would be 'dominant' in bed. In Chapter Three, we will take a look at some advertising that is mentioned by some of the female informants as representing masculine sexuality.

(6)   Masculinity Over the Life Cycle

Another aspect of masculinity seemingly overlooked by prior marketing research is that the meaning and manifestation of the concept changes over the life cycle of the man. Young, unmarried men see masculinity in terms of personal adventures, competitions and triumphs. These may be fights they have won, women they have bedded, and sports victories—often the winnings are viewed as 'trophies.' In particular, these exploits seem to be viewed as more meaningful if the foe, task or obstacle is particularly dangerous, difficult or challenging.

The descriptions of these activities given by those to whom we talked are somewhat reminiscent of a gunfighter carving notches on his gun, athletes recounting seconds shaved off a prior record or the number of home runs hit in a season. In this youthful form of masculinity, it is important to keep score and to discuss the difficulty of the conditions or the strength of the opponents, as this places the accomplishment in proper context for admiration by others, for example, "He threw a no-hitter with tendonitis in his elbow"; "he crawled the last 400 yards with a broken leg and frostbite."

It is not just the final score but also the demands of the course that contribute to the sense of manliness in a given field of endeavor. Even losing to an enormously superior opponent can be viewed as masculine, because the contender had the courage to take on an unwinnable task—better to lose nobly than stand meekly on the sidelines.

Older men, those who fought, won and lost multiple battles in their youth and are now married with children, have a different perspective. At this point in their lives, masculinity signifies responsibility, maturity and 'doing the right thing' for their families. To some extent, their manliness is tested by *resisting* the temptation to take large physical or financial risks that might have been very attractive in earlier years. A mature masculine man avoids the narcissism of showboating and gambling with assets that his family needs to live well.

Recall the words in Chapter One from the coal miner's son who told of how his father "worked sick, tired, hurt" to provide a living for his family—this was a man who was a champion football player in high school and surely enjoyed the respect of men and the adulation of women that came with that status in a small rural town. Now the greatest evidence of his continuing masculinity is his willingness to sacrifice himself for the welfare of his family. His son recognizes this as his father's legacy and will likely carry it forward in his own life.

Figure 2.6 Photograph of high school football player. The high school football player who carries the ball across the goal line is an icon of masculinity for many young men.

Source: Tinnell, Jeff. *SETH* RUN *vs Idalou.* 2005. *Wikimedia Commons.* Web. 25 Aug. 2015.

https://commons.wikimedia.org/wiki/File:SETH_RUN_vs_idalou.jpg

Figure 2.7 Photograph of middle-aged coal miners at work. The adult realities of many working-class men include a stoic, self-sacrificing aspect of masculinity.

Source: Everett Historical. *Coal Miners.* Digital Image. Shutterstock. 14 Feb 1926. Web. 03 Sept. 2015.

(7)   Masculinity as a Transitional Status between Nature and Culture

I am going to end this chapter with a discussion of two characters from one of humankind's earliest myths. The *Epic of Gilgamesh* was first recorded in written form in early Sumer (ca. 2500 BCE) and is a favorite of mine because it serves as a semiotic Ur-myth (*the* Ur-myth) for all the symbol-laden narratives on masculinity which have postdated it through the millennia. The two men in the story are Enkidu, a wild man who lives in the forest, and Gilgamesh, the king of Uruk. Enkidu represents the 'natural state' of man. He is strong, handsome, hair covered, does not shave, has long head hair, drinks from streams and grazes on grass. He can relate to animals, running with them and protecting them. (We see direct echoes of Enkidu in Edgar Rice Burroughs's character Tarzan.)

Over time, he becomes the best friend of King Gilgamesh, who sends a temple prostitute to teach Enkidu the ways of sexuality. Once introduced to the pleasures of female companionship and human society, Enkidu joins Gilgamesh on many adventures requiring courage, strength and intelligence.

If we view Enkidu and Gilgamesh as two sides of human manhood, we come to better understand the conceptual structure of masculinity. Enkidu is the dirty, hairy, animal-like aspect of masculinity, the part of maleness that can survive in the wild, that is not afraid of being alone in the wilderness, who can "live off the land," as one of our interviewees put it. Gilgamesh is the civilized aspect of masculinity; the part of maleness that can lead other men into battle, dominate social interactions, organize military campaigns and take charge of political and financial resources. Both are adept at surviving and prospering *in their respective domains*—and notably, the story suggests that both aspects of masculinity are necessary to complete the adventures they set out on. Masculinity requires dual 'tool sets'—the wild and the urbane.

The persons to whom we spoke seemed to grasp this notion intuitively, no doubt a result of having grown up in contemporary America. The masculinity they describe implicitly incorporates the ability to navigate between raw, violent, dangerous natural events and the requirements of organized society, which can also contain raw, violent and dangerous challenges. Masculine men are those capable of transporting the dirty, the dangerous and the disordered away from their families and out of society and concurrently of bringing the valuable and useful back from treacherous, chaotic places to their families and into society. To do so, they must be competent and confident in two worlds, never retreating completely into one or the other.

3   What Women Want

When asked "What does masculinity mean to you?," the women to whom we spoke voiced beliefs similar to those given by men. For example, a typical response is:

> *Being a man. It's what kind of man you are. Physically when I think of a masculine body it is not someone who is puny or skinny. He has a deeper voice. Big hands, big feet, hair on the chest and under the armpits. Someone that eats meat. Mentally, it would be someone who is respectful, a gentleman. Runs the house . . . Number one thing I think about for masculinity is the word 'mature.'*
>
> (Female, age 22, Northeast, unmarried)

When describing what their fathers would think was masculine, a typical response by women is,

> *A man's man. Strong. Someone who can take care of the wife and kids, protect you. Do stuff around the house, fixing things. . . . Providing for the family. Being confident . . . would take a bullet for his family, knows how to sacrifice.*
>
> (Female, age 35, Southeast, married with children)

However, despite the large overlap in perceptions, there are some intriguing differences that will be discussed in this chapter: Women added details to the physical descriptions of masculinity that were not mentioned as often by men. Among these are that masculine men are *taller* than most men. They have deeper voices, "have to shave in the morning" and "are handsome." In these descriptions, women appear to be emphasizing the desirability of the masculine man as a potential mate—something that was not present in the interviews with men. Evolutionary theorists propose that women do consciously or unconsciously seek out mates who exhibit protectiveness and physical strength and attractive features (see, e.g., Buss 1994).

Bear with me for a moment as I discuss current thinking in human evolutionary science on mate choice—the result will be worth it for men who want a

Figure 3.1 Photograph of Arnold Schwarzenegger. Evolutionary research indicates that women prefer men with strong brow ridges, prominent chins and muscular torsos during the fertile period of their estrus cycle. Actor Arnold Schwarzenegger has personified the characteristics in several motion pictures, most memorably the *Terminator* series.

Source: Featureflash. *Gov. Arnold Schwarzenegger*. Digital Image. Shutterstock. 13 Dec. 2006. Web. 03 Sept. 2015.

Figure 3.2 Photograph of Matthew McConaughey and Channing Tatum. Actors Matthew McConaughey and Channing Tatum are current icons of the masculine physique.

Source: Esteb, Helga. *Matthew McConaughey, Channing Tatum.* Digital Image. Shutterstock. 24 June 2012. Web. 03 Sept. 2015.

better understanding of what women are looking for. Among animals (of which we are an exemplar species), females exhibit a strong evolutionary bias toward exaggerated male traits (e.g., Andersson 1994; Zahavi 1975). Among these are length of males' tail feathers in some bird species, bright colors in other bird species, pack dominance among wild dogs, fighting ability among caribou, size and strength among elephants, and so forth. As Folstad and Karter (1992) and Hamilton and Zuk (1982) report, these overt signals of physical health are linked to genetically based immunocompetence—the ability to resist infection by parasites in the local ecosystem. This turns out to be hereditable in the offspring of the males. As Geary, Virgil and Byrd-Craven (2003, p. 28) put it, "Male ornaments are barometers that are strongly affected by the condition of the male, and female mate choices reflect the *evolution of females' ability to read these barometers.*"

Over the millennia during which humans have been living in settled groups, social cognitions have also evolved so that cultural cues are used by human females to guide their mate choices. In contemporary society, this means that women look for men who not only can endow their children with outstanding physical traits but also exhibit socially desirable traits such as high income earnings, upward social mobility, intelligence, high-status possessions, sexual fidelity and emotional support for the children (Buss 1994; Irons 1983). On top of this, contemporary women also (of course) want their mates to be physically capable of protecting them and the children, as well as sexually and emotionally compatible (see, e.g., Geary and Flinn 2001).

This is a tall order! If any readers watched the long-running television series *Sex and the City*, they are aware that women discuss the trade-offs involved in human female mate selection in great detail. They fantasize about (and occasionally bed) their masculine dream man (e.g., David Beckham, Mikhail Baryshnikov), but often 'settle for' the safe man who will be a good provider. The only women who seem to be capable of mating long term with a masculine man who is also rich, famous and madly in love with them and their children are those who, themselves, are the alpha females of the time period. Perhaps the premier example of this currently is the Brad Pitt–Angelina Jolie coupling.

Adding support to this interpretation is the presence of multiple mentions by women of the importance of masculine men's sexual prowess. They are described as "taking the lead in sex," being "good in bed," "virile" and "sexually dominant." Several women mentioned the men in the Calvin Klein underwear ads and also the several appearances of soccer star David Beckham in underwear ads.

What these images have in common is a male model, often with facial stubble, an unsmiling, even somber, demeanor, a very fit physique—often with tattoos—and large genitals tightly tucked into a small pair of underwear. Obviously, there is a lot of sexual promise in such images, and many women seemed to find them very attractive. (Returning to our Enkidu example from the previous chapter, this is likely what Donna Summer meant in her disco song "Hot Stuff" when she stated, "I want to bring a wild man back home.") Notably, none of the men to whom we spoke mentioned this type of advertising, perhaps because to do so could suggest they were gay.

Related to this seems to be the tendency of women to mention more *media-based models* of masculinity than did men. The women we interviewed are also more likely to mention particular motion picture or television show characters as representing masculinity; examples here would include Channing Tatum in *Magic Mike* and Matthew McConaughey (in virtually anything except *Dallas Buyers Club*). This suggests the possibility that many women may obtain their ideas (and ideals) of masculinity from mass media, because they do not 'hang out' with men as frequently or in the same contexts that men do. For instance, they don't hang out at bars drinking with male friends, don't play contact sports with men, don't go hunting or fishing with men—all the ways in which men learn about other men and masculinity. As a result, women likely are more dependent on media images because they lack direct contact experience. (It would be interesting to see if men have a similarly restricted set of images for conceptualizing femininity.)

Women differed also in placing more emphasis on a masculine man's having *professional job status*. They saw masculine men as having careers and being able to provide financial security for the family. Some specifically mentioned they liked masculine men in suits, which to them represented "confidence, wealth, responsibility and a position in top management." This, of course, is very consistent with evolutionary psychologist David Buss's research

Figure 3.3 Photograph of a handsome, well-dressed businessman. Women want a man who is cool in the boardroom and hot in the bedroom.

Source: El Nariz. *Businessman*. Digital Image. Shutterstock. Web. 03 Sept. 2015.

indicating that contemporary women often seek to exchange their beauty and fertility for a potential husband's job status and financial assets (and see also Hirschman 1989).

A final divergence between the men and women to whom we talked is in the area of brand-relevant knowledge. Very interestingly, women, despite often being labeled as the family shoppers, were substantially less cognizant of men's brands than were the men in the sample. For example, women named the same product *categories* representing masculinity as men, for example weapons, vehicles, grooming products, alcohol, tools, but they recited far fewer *brands*. Indeed, they seemed reliant on the *most advertised* men's brands, such as Budweiser beer, Calvin Klein underwear, Axe and Old Spice deodorant, Nike shoes, Gillette razors, Hanes underwear. They did not name, for instance, Craftsman tools, Mustang cars, Jameson whisky, DeWalt tools, Guinness ale, or Mossy Oak hunting gear. Their brand knowledge seems to be limited to those brands most widely advertised nationally. They lack expertise in the intricate details of men's branding. This finding could be of significance to the marketers of men's products who would like for women to include their brands on gift lists for their husbands or boyfriends.

4   Masculinity as a Vehicle

Get your motor runnin'
Head out on the highway
Lookin' for adventure
and whatever comes our way.
Like a true nature's child.
We were born, born to be wild.
. . . Born to be wild!
Born to be wild!
("Born to Be Wild," Steppenwolf, 1969)

I would like to have a 1993 Ford Mustang Cobra as a Sunday drive car . . . I would drive out and show off during spring and summer weather. I would take . . . $20,000 and sink it into the restoration and upgrade process on the Mustang. I would also like to have an SUV that is big enough for a family of seven. I want it to be top of the line . . . dependable as well as safe. I would also like a Chevy Silver King Cab with larger than factory tires, running boards, a lift kit and a tool box. If I couldn't have that. . . . a Ford F-150 Raptor . . . The Raptor would be better because of the engine size and power.
(Josh, age 28, Southeast, married with two children)

In this chapter, we are going to make our first venture into specific brands and product categories. The product category under discussion is motor vehicles, and the three brands to be examined are Harley-Davidson motorcycles, Ford pickup trucks and Ford Mustang automobiles. These three brands were dominant across age levels and regions as representing masculinity. I will argue that each has a unique history and role to play in representing American masculinity.

Because I am female, I had some knowledge about each of these brands but did not possess the deep knowledge that a man growing up in the United States would likely possess. This likely proved beneficial, because I was able to read through the voluminous literature on each of these brands with fresh, naive eyes, perhaps seeing cues and clues that would be so deeply embedded in a man's psyche that they would not surface.

As described in what follows, I believe each of these brands is seen as masculine for different reasons and carries with it a different set of cultural associations. For example, the Harley-Davidson motorcycle brand represents rebelliousness, freedom, independence from social expectations and conventions, yet at the same time draws on the male impulse to be part of a 'pack.' Harley riders usually do not go out on solitary adventures; rather they draw their male strength from numbers, belonging to a large, potentially violent group capable of wreaking havoc on a community. Riding together, they can "become Death, the Destroyer of Worlds" (to quote Robert Oppenheimer and *Bhagavad Vita*).

Conversely, Ford pickup drivers are masculine because they make solitary journeys between civilization and the wilderness. They haul cultural debris into the wilderness and in turn haul valuable pieces of nature (e.g., firewood, calves, slain deer) back to their homes. The pickup truck is the iconic vehicle for this dual-delivery function. In particular, the Ford F-150 series has come to signify the essence of this type of vehicle. It is the category prototype, although Chevrolet and Dodge are close behind.

The third brand, Ford Mustang, is the surviving member of the 1960s phenomenon of the 'muscle car.' Mustang began and continues as the category prototype for the American stock sports car. In researching its origins and representation in popular culture media as well as advertising, it became apparent that the Mustang signals a different aspect of masculinity than the other two brands of vehicles men named. The Mustang is used to signal other men of one's aggressiveness, competitiveness and dominance. More than the Harley-Davidson motorcycle or the Ford pickup truck, it is a statement of self-identity and public posing. A man rides in it to show off for women and to attract the envy of other men. The Mustang symbolizes the social stature of one's masculinity.

Harley-Davidson Motorcycles

Although Harley-Davidson motorcycles have been manufactured since 1905, they did not enter the public consciousness as vehicles of masculinity until after World War II. They were *pre-positioned* to be carriers of masculinity by a 1930 Howard Hughes film, *Hells Angels*, which followed the war time careers of two RAF pilots stationed in France during World War I. Before setting off on a suicide mission to bomb a German munitions depot, the pilots venture into town one last time to say goodbye to a girlfriend (played by the 'original blonde bombshell', Jean Harlow). They ride on a black Harley-Davidson motorcycle emblazoned with a skull pierced by an arrow (which, of course, was later adopted as the emblem of the California motorcycle gang Hell's Angels).

Harley-Davidson built 80,000 motorcycles for use by Allied troops in World War II. When the American soldiers who rode these vehicles returned home after the war,

> many of them returned with only the skills they'd acquired in the army. They could make war, fix motorcycles, and ride them well . . . . The country was grateful, but there were no jobs . . . . They had little to do and few prospects . . . Most of these young men took what remained of their war pay . . . and bought motorcycles . . . With no families, they didn't need cars . . . These men became bitter and restless, once the heroes' welcome had worn off.
>
> (Leffingwell 1996, p. 77)

By the late 1940s, the American Motorcycle Association formed a Gypsy Tour that held competitive dirt-track races at venues across the country—many were in California because of the warm climate and the prevalence of young discharged soldiers. Leffingwell (1996, p. 78) writes, "Gasoline was cheap and so was the beer. Hotels were sparse . . . so when hundreds of racing enthusiasts rode into town, there were never enough places for them to eat, sleep or care for themselves."

On July 4th weekend 1947, a group of 4,000 motorcycle riders and their hangers-on rode into Hollister, California, for a racing competition at Veterans Park, a 1/3 mile dirt track. Several began racing each other on the main street of Hollister near a bar called Johnny's. Many were members of an Oakland motorcycle club called the Booze Fighters. Too much alcohol was consumed; fights broke out; property was destroyed and about fifty people were arrested by the Hollister police force. A reporter from the San Francisco *Chronicle* went to the scene and took an iconic photograph of a large, belligerent, drunk Harley rider parked in front of Johnny's bar.

Life magazine featured the photograph on its cover that week, together with a story claiming that the town of Hollister had been attacked by a drunken horde of motorcycle riders who had wrecked the town, sexually assaulted several women and generally raised hell. The Harley myth was born. It was embellished substantially by director/producer Stanley Kramer in his 1953 film *The Wild One*. Starring Marlon Brando and Lee Marvin, the narrative depicted two rival motorcycle gangs led by Brando and Marvin, respectively.

Brando played the antihero of the film, one of the first iconically mixed characters to appear in American cinema, while Marvin played the more sinister, predatory biker. Marvin rode the Harley. Aligned semiotically with the motorcycle menace were jazz music, jukeboxes, black leather and sexuality. When Brando's character takes the virginal blonde heroine on a ride, she tells him, "I've never ridden on a motorcycle before . . . It's fast. It scared me. But I forgot everything. It felt good. Is that what you do?"

In 1956, Elvis Presley, also symbolic of youthful rebellion, sexuality and a dangerous new musical form, rock 'n roll, purchased a Harley and had a publicity photo taken with him astride it.

Thus, entering the 1960s, Harley-Davidson had become an icon of danger, rebellion and sexuality to young men (and their admiring women) throughout the United States. The decade of the sixties saw the enshrinement of the motorcycle, and especially Harley-Davidson, as the preferred vehicle of the wild, dangerous, sexualized male. Books from the time period carried titles such as *Run Tough, Run Hard, The Death Cycle, The Devil's Rider, The Black Leather Barbarians* and *The Bike from Hell*. Movies included such features as *Devil Rider*, which promised "the cycle jungle of hot flesh and raw steel . . . Blood and Guts and Outlaws on Wheels!"

In 1968, the Rolling Stones—the evil idols of rock and roll—performed at Altamont Speedway in California. The gathering, often termed the anti-Woodstock, was marked by drugs, drunkenness, sexual assaults and one murder. The Stones were escorted to the stage by a phalanx of Hell's Angels aboard their Harley 'choppers' in full denim jacket/death's head regalia. One of the Angels stabbed an out-of-control man to death in front of the stage as Jagger was performing "Under My Thumb."

Counter-culture journalists of the period called upon imagery that would cement the iconography surrounding Harley motorcycles into the national psyche.

> The concept of the motorcycle outlaw was as uniquely American as jazz. Nothing like them ever existed before. . . . They appeared a kind of half-breed anachronism, a human hangover from the . . . Wild West. California, Labor Day Weekend . . . outlaw motorcyclists wearing chains, shades and greasy Levi's roll out from damp garages, all night diners and cast-off one-night pads in Frisco, Hollywood, Berdoo and East Oakland . . . The Menace is loose again.
>
> (Thompson 1967, p. 5)

> It was like a locomotive about 10 miles away. It was the Hell's Angels in running formation coming over the mountain on Harley-Davidson 74s. THRAGGGGGH . . . and the locomotive sound got louder and louder until you couldn't near yourself talk anymore. . . . Here they come around the last curve. The Hells Angels with the bikes, the beards, the long hair, the sleeveless denim jackets with the death's head insignia.
>
> (Wolfe 1968, p. 79)

And then in 1969 came *Easy Rider.* Starring Peter Fonda and Dennis Hopper, with Jack Nicholson along for part of the ride, this film featured customized Harleys. Nicholson, as a drunken small-town lawyer who decided, fatefully, to ride with them, gave the soliloquy that aptly summed up one of the core masculinity concepts symbolized by the Harley:

> What you represent to them is freedom . . . Talking about it and being it are two different things. It's real hard to be free when you are bought and sold in the marketplace. . . . They see a free individual, it's gonna scare 'em.
>
> (Jack Nicholson as George Hanson in *Easy Rider* [1969])

That night, Nicholson is beaten to death with baseball bats by local towns-people as the trio camp out along a roadside. The characters played by Fonda and Hopper, Captain America and Billy, are later slain on a rural highway in the Southeast by two men who represent a different form of masculinity—the kind that carries hunting rifles and drives pickup trucks.

Headlines from a series of Harley-Davidson advertisements that span several decades include: "Carve your name on Blacktop," "Only one man could have done this," "The Dream of every red-blooded American" and "Unleash your dark side."

In my view, Leffingwell (1995, p. 171) sums up the masculinity of Harley-Davidson motorcycles most accurately:

> More than any other product made by humans, Harley owners ride for the brand. No one tattoos Buick Electra or IBM or Rolex or Sony Trinitron or Steinway across their chest or back . . . . Harley-Davidson is like a brand burned into the calf's flank. It has a loyalty unmatched by any other product and envied by most. . . . Imagine what would happen if hundreds of Harley-Davidsons rode over the San Andreas Fault all at once. Prudence would dictate an east bound route (toward Reno and Phoenix). But Prudence doesn't ride a Harley.

Figure 4.1 Photograph of Harley-Davidson brand symbol. The Harley-Davidson brand symbol shows a fierce American eagle in attack position. The slogan "Live to Ride" calls men to the freedom of the open road.

Source: Kohl, Sergey. *Berlin, Germany.* Digital Image. Shutterstock. Web. 03 Sept. 2015

Figure 4.2 Silhouette photograph of the Harley-Davidson motorcycle. Gleaming metal and motor dominated, the Harley-Davidson motorcycle is simultaneously a military tank and a knight's charger; the 'chopper' accompanies its rider in battle and on heroic quests.

Source: Armyagov, Andrey. *Harley-Davidson.* Digital Image. Shutterstock. 07 July 2013. Web. 03 Sept. 2015.

Ford: The Iconic Pickup Truck

We now turn to the second of our trio of iconic masculine vehicles—the Ford pickup truck and most specifically the Ford F-150 model. In 1969 as *Easy Rider*s Captain America and Billy were crossing America on their custom Harley cycles, they ran smack dab into an even earlier masculine vehicle, the rural pickup truck. Driven by two middle-aged good ol' boys, the battered dark green Ford F-100 was the workhouse of rural America, especially in the Southeastern region. On the back window hung a gun rack carrying a loaded shotgun. As the rebellious, outlaw bikers drove by, the two farmers in the truck swerved toward them and fired two shots, killing the long-haired hippies on board the cycles. It was a perfect moment of cinematic conflict between two sets of cultural ideology about manhood and two vehicles used to signify it.

The pickup truck was originated by Henry Ford in 1917 as a one-ton Model TT. By 1948, Ford had upgraded its utility and design and introduced the F-1 model truck, which is the predecessor of the current F-150, F-250 and F-350 pickup designs. Chevrolet and Dodge Motor Companies provided consistent competition to Ford in the marketplace with their pickup models, Chevrolet even leading Ford from 1938 to 1968 (Mueller 2008). By 1997, Ford had sold 26 million F-style pickups in the United States, making it the most popular brand of automotive vehicle *worldwide*.

Figure 4.3 Photograph of Ford F-150 in an automobile showroom. The enormous grille and high, wide front end of the Ford F-150 exude dominance on the road and masculine power under the hood.

Source: Brode, Darren. Digital Image. Shutterstock. 12 Jan 2015. Web. 03 Sept. 2015.

Along the way, the F-150 evolved from a rural utility vehicle to a flashy, air-conditioned, Dolby-stereo-system–equipped, chrome-laden behemoth with heated leather seats, weighing in at 1.5 tons and generating 300+ horsepower with a V8 engine. The rural 'workhorse' had become a showy stallion.

As Mueller writes, (2008, p. 116), "Image consciousness gained prominence during the Sixties . . . [There was] a growing preference for the trendy Styleside body . . . Even more style and flair became available in 1965 by way of the new Ranger package . . . According to Ford this option was 'designed to appeal to the luxury and sports minded light truck operator.'" Mag wheel covers were drawn from the popular entry of the muscle car era of the 1960s and 1970s (as we shall see in detail when discussion turns to the Ford Mustang). The masculine meaning of the pickup truck, especially in its full-size, fully tricked-out version, evolved from *workhorse* to *show horse*. Power, engine size, height and hauling capacity became ways of demonstrating one's masculine presence to others on the road. A Ford brochure from 2004 for the F-150 declares that the new model was meant to "communicate a tough visual strength with boldness and honesty" (Mueller 2008, p. 143).

In a match likely made in a venue other than Heaven (Hell, most likely), the ultimate macho mating took place—the Harley-Davidson Ford F-150 was born bearing the Harley-Davidson winged logo with a midnight-black interior and exterior finish, 20-inch, five-spoke chromed wheels and a 'power plant' capable of generating 340 horsepower.

Motor Trend magazine said of the 2003 model, "The Ford F-150 Harley-Davidson Edition sets a high standard for tough-truck styling and backs that up with 340 supercharged horsepower. The result is a pickup with catapult-like thrust and Lincoln-grade appointments." The H-D edition carried forward through the next decade and extended to the larger size F-250 and F-350 pickup offerings. Clearly, the concept of masculinity the Ford-Harley truck embodies has morphed into a statement of power and prestige, in addition to the danger and utility implied by the earlier Harley motorcycles and F-series Ford pickups, respectively. The irony here is that the enormous, costly and exquisitely appointed H-D-F model pickup has lost its ability both to work in the dirty, dusty, gravel-road environment from which its pickup ancestors came and to provide the no-cares, no-responsibility, repair-it-on-the-side-of-the-road freedom the Harley cycles represented.

Howard Zehr (2013) conducted interviews with several pickup owners in the Southeastern United States. Most of them drive Fords, but some have Chevy Silverados and Dodge Rams. Excerpts from these interviews are given in what follows to illustrate the split between the pickup-as-workhorse and the pickup-as-show-horse theme introduced earlier.

My white truck is a 2000 Ford F-250 Super Duty with a nine-inch lift kit and a V10 motor. There are blue neon lights that light up the whole underneath and the whole inside wheel area is red. And it has a boomin', boomin' stereo system.

(Kelly Randolph, Virginia)

I pulled stuff with my old truck: cattle trailers, horse trailers, trailers with hay in them. I made it do the job. I trusted it, I believed in it, and it did it. This one here, I can pull trailers. . . . and I feel like it looks good. I have a very big problem with driving a vehicle that doesn't look good. . . . I use my truck to express myself . . . a statement to rub in everyone's faces . . . They see my truck and they're like "Oh boy, he's doin' good for himself." I sit back and just smile. . . . So far I've changed the headlights, revamped the interior. And put in Mossy Oak floor mats, windshield visor and sun-screen, ... I'm gonna do everything to make it the biggest and best, the strongest kid on the playground. People look at my truck and say, "that's one bad-ass Chevrolet."

I mainly coon hunt with dogs. I used to bear hunt a good bit, but I don't have as much time . . . My license plate stands for Bluetick—that's the kind of dogs I use. They love riding back there . . . I love the outdoors, and that's what I use this truck for. I'm just a truck guy . . . I like to have something there if you gotta haul something . . . I might go in the mountains or anywhere.

(Robert Fulk)

The Ford Mustang

The third vehicle named by those to whom we talked as consistently representing masculinity is the Ford Mustang. The Mustang burst onto the cultural landscape in 1964 in an explosion of publicity and advertising. Both *Time* and *Newsweek* gave the new car line cover stories. The Mustang was displayed at the World's Fair in New York City on April 17, 1964, taking its position in the pantheon of global accomplishments alongside Belgian Village and the Unisphere.

Topping off this celebratory extravaganza, the Mustang was driven by Miss Pussy Galore, James Bond's girlfriend in the top film of 1964, *Goldfinger*. Now that was a brand launch!

By the end of 1965, Ford had sold 2,000,000 Mustangs, the most successful automotive launch in history. But perhaps the crowning achievement cementing the machismo of the Mustang in its early years was the archetypal 9-minute, 42-second car chase in the film *Bullitt* (1968), when man's man actor Steve McQueen drove a Ford Mustang and outmaneuvered the bad guys, who were driving a Dodge Charger.

Ford's introductory advertising print campaign emphasized the European elegance of the car, coupled with the promise of muscle car power under the hood. American males were filled with lust! In my view, the Mustang has succeeded in remaining an icon of masculinity across the generations by continuously linking its street cars to high-performance racing vehicles—providing every man who drives one the ability to fantasize that he is not on an interstate highway or two-lane blacktop road but rather is Carroll Shelby at LeMans, Steve Saleen at the Trans Am finals or one of Jack Roush's NASCAR drivers, Matt Kenseth, Jeff Burton or Carl Edwards. Then there is always the

Figure 4.4 Photograph of Mustang GT. Every aspect of the Mustang's design evokes forward thrust, aggressiveness and masculine drive.

Source: Kohl, Sergey. *Shelby GT 500E Super Snake*. Digital Image. Shutterstock. 10 May 2015. Web. 03 Sept. 2015.

fantasy of being Parnelli Jones, who drove a Grabber Orange Boss 302 Mustang to victory in multiple Trans Am races.

The Mustang, more than any other car in America, has permitted men to imagine themselves as racecar drivers. It forms a perfect trifecta with the wild, dark freedom of the Harley-Davidson cycle and the 'natural man' aura of the Ford F-150 pickup: competition, violence, wilderness—three arenas in which men believe they have to prove themselves. The Shelby Cobra Mustang symbol perhaps sums up these three domains—and bears a striking (pun intended) resemblance to an erect male penis.

5 Weapons

I was born and raised on a farm in Texas and have been interested in guns and hunting as long as I can remember. Some of my earliest memories are of me tagging along with Dad as he hunted doves with his single-shot 20-gauge. My job was to pick up the birds and put them in a paper bag . . . I learned to shoot with that Eastern Arms 20-gauge and Dad's Remington 521T bolt-action 22. Soon I got my own .22 (a Winchester model 67) and did my best to eradicate the jackrabbit population in central Texas. . . . With those three guns I made frequent contributions to the dinner table with doves, squirrels and quail. I got my first deer with a borrowed .30–.30 when I was 16. In the ensuing years I have hunted deer, antelope, upland game and waterfowl in several states, but to this day my favorite hunting memories are from those days on the farm.

(Lee 2013, p. 5)

Go ahead; make my day.

(actor Clint Eastwood as Detective Harry Callahan in
Sudden Impact [1983], pointing a Smith & Wesson
.44 magnum handgun at a criminal)

Virtually every man to whom we spoke named Smith & Wesson firearms as a masculine brand. Those men we interviewed living in the Southeastern region of the county also named Remington and Winchester rifles as masculine brands. The difference in response patterns between the two regions is due to the fact that hunting is a very common part of the male experience in the Southeast (see, e.g., Littlefield and Ozanne 2011). Boys are typically taught by their fathers to use firearms and go hunting; thus, guns are seen as a normal part of the male environment. Conversely, in urban and suburban portions of the Northeast, guns, especially long guns and shotguns, are very rare. There is no tradition of firearms use or hunting. Thus, how do Northeastern men learn about firearms? They watch male-oriented movies and television shows.

Among these media exemplars of masculine firearms use, Clint Eastwood's character of Dirty Harry Callahan reigns supreme. Clint Eastwood also made several westerns using Winchester and Remington rifles and Colt .45 handguns,

Figure 5.1 Actor James Arness as Marshal Matt Dillon. The television series *Gunsmoke* starring James Arness as Marshal Matt Dillon was one of the most popular shows of all time. Generations of young American boys grew up viewing Marshal Dillon as their hero. Dillon was the boundary between order and chaos.

Source: CBS Television. *James Arness Gunsmoke 1974.* 1974. *Wikimedia Commons.* Web. 25 Aug. 2015

https://commons.wikimedia.org/wiki/File:James_Arness_Gunsmoke_1974.JPG

as did John Wayne, Gary Cooper, Jimmy Stewart, Guy Madison, James Arness, James Garner, Richard Boone and more recently Kurt Russell, Kevin Costner and even Jamie Fox (*Django Unchained*).

Handguns and rifles have been used by American men since Colonial times, and target shooting and hunting are still very common in the rural areas of the United States. What is it about firearms that makes them so masculine? Undoubtedly the primary attribute is that they enable the user to shoot someone else (e.g., an intruder, an enemy, a victim) or something else (e.g., a game animal or predator animal). In one aspect, guns should be seen as *less* masculine than fighting with a knife or sword or hand-to-hand combat, because they remove the need for physical superiority from the fight (and size and strength are viewed as masculine). But they seem to compensate for this by carrying more destructive force than blades or fists. A hollow-point round can destroy an enemy with a single shot. As Harry Callahan told one criminal in *Dirty Harry*, "This .44 Smith & Wesson is the most powerful gun made . . . It can blow your head right off." The opponent surrendered.

Remington and Winchester Rifles

We are going to start our analysis by taking a look at the two oldest firearms companies still operating in the United States—Remington and Winchester. Notably, both these brands are mentioned by the editor of *Gun Digest 2013* (Lee 2013) quoted at the opening to this chapter as ones he used as a child. Remington is the older of the two companies, having been founded by the son of a commercial iron foundry owner in upstate New York in 1816. His first product was a flintlock rifle, then the predominant model of firearm in the newly formed United States. By the late 1840s, Remington Arms was doing a booming business selling rifles to arm US soldiers in a war with Mexico.

Remington's core competency was the development of mass-produced interchangeable parts, which enabled spare and repair parts to be made available for all rifles they manufactured. By the Civil War (in which their arms were used by both Union troops and the Confederate Army) their factory in New York was making 200 pistols and 1,000 rifles per day—a total that reached 40,000 muskets, 12,500 rifles, 144,000 revolvers and 20,000 carbines by the end of the war. This turned out to be a remarkable boon for the Remington brand, as after the war, discharged soldiers on both sides carried their Remingtons westward with the country's expansion into new territories. The availability of spare parts kept these firearms in operation for decades.

Remington produced 1.5 million Enfield model rifles for British and American troops in World War I—which then came home with the returning troops and entered private collections,

> keeping the Remington brand in the cultural consciousness. During World War II, Remington again produced rifles, and ammunition, for Allied troops supplying over 1,000,000 firearms of various sizes and models. And once again, these firearms returned with the discharged soldiers at the end of the war. At this point, the Remington brand had reached a saturation level in the American male consciousness as 'the' firearm to carry.

Figure 5.2 Civil War painting of Union soldiers on the field. Both the Union and Confederate armies made use of Remington firearms during the Civil War. The durability of the Remington made it one of the most often-used weapons in the movement westward after the Civil War.

Source: Troiani, Don. *General of the Confederacy.* 2012. *Wikimedia Commons.* Web. 25 Aug. 2015

https://commons.wikimedia.org/wiki/File:General_of_the_Confederacy.jpg

The Winchester Arms Company was established in Connecticut in 1866 and manufactured both rifles and pistols; by 1897, it had developed a repeating shotgun and a self-loading rifle in 1905. Though it missed being an arms supplier to Civil War combatants, Winchester did manufacture Enfield model rifles for both the United States and Britain in World War I and the Garand M-1 rifle for the US military in World War II. More than half a million Garand M-1s were

Figure 5.3 Early print advertisement for Remington rifle. This advertisement for the Remington rifle notes its ability to make multiple rapid-fire shots.

Source: Internet Archive Book Images. *Image from page 389 of "Breeder and Sportsman" (1882).* 1882. San Francisco Public Library, California. *Wikimedia Commons.* Web. 25 Aug. 2015.

https://commons.wikimedia.org/wiki/File:Image_from_page_389_of_%22Breeder_and_sports man%22_(1882)_(14784843942).jpg

Figure 5.4 Photograph of managers at Remington Firearms Company. These two managers at Remington's headquarters discuss the multiple-shot chamber capability of the firearm.

Source: World War I US Army Signal Corps Collection. *Browning with his BAR.* 1918. *Wikimedia Commons.* Web. 25 Aug. 2015.

https://commons.wikimedia.org/wiki/File:Browning_with_his_BAR.jpg

Figure 5.5 1874 photograph of Buffalo Bill Cody. This remarkable photograph of Buffalo Bill Cody dates from 1874 and shows him holding his Winchester rifle. Cody is clad in iconic Western outdoorsman apparel, including buckskin jacket, leather riding gloves and high leather riding boots. Behind him rests his saddle, while a rope lies at this feet.

Source: Burke-K. *Buffalo Bill Cody by Burke (1982)*. 1892. Illinois. *Wikimedia Commons*. Web. 25 Aug. 2015.

https://commons.wikimedia.org/wiki/File:Buffalo_Bill_Cody_by_Burke,_1892.jpg

produced; most are now in civilian collections. Perhaps the two most culturally resonant images of the brand are a photograph of President Theodore Roosevelt holding his Winchester rifle while dressed in fringed buckskin hunting apparel and an 1874 photograph of Buffalo Bill Cody with his Winchester rifle.

Winchester's slogan, "The gun that won the west," is coupled with an armed cowboy on a galloping horse image in much of its advertising during the twentieth century.

Smith & Wesson

After the Civil War ended, settlers moved into the great expanse of the American West. Native Americans, into whose tribal lands they were migrating, began systematic attacks on the arriving whites. The US Cavalry was assigned to protect these settlers and set up a series of forts along the ever-widening western border (cites). Smith & Wesson Armory of Springfield, Massachusetts, was chosen to supply the Cavalry with revolvers. The S&W Model 3, which used a .44 cartridge, became the standard-issue cavalry gun and soon had diffused into the consumer market as well. The Model 3 was durable, reliable and accurate—the three most vital characteristics for a handgun in the West.

Figure 5.6 Photograph of Smith & Wesson Model 3 .44-caliber handgun. This Model 3 Smith & Wesson handgun is beautifully engraved with filigree and an image of Diana, the goddess of the hunt, and her dogs.

Source: Cumpston. *Mountaingun2006.* 2007. *Wikimedia Commons.* Web. 25 Aug. 2015.

https://commons.wikimedia.org/wiki/File:Mountaingun2006.jpg

Smith & Wesson became *the* handgun of choice for the famed figures of the Old West—on both sides of the law. They were carried by Frank and Jesse James, Cole Younger, Texas Jack, Virgil Earp, John Wesley Hardin, Wild Bill Hickok, Pat Garrett, Buffalo Bill Cody and Teddy Roosevelt (Boorman 2002). With 'brand spokespersons' such as these, the masculinity of the weapon was guaranteed.

Although Clint Eastwood's character, Dirty Harry Callahan, popularized the Smith & Wesson .44 for the present generation of men, the Smith & Wesson .38 model was carried a generation earlier by Sergeant Joe Friday and Officer Bill Gannon in the very popular television series *Dragnet* of the 1950s. As if this were not sufficient testosterone for the Smith & Wesson reputation, General George S. Patton carried his .357 Magnum during World War II.

Figure 5.7 Photograph of Frank and Jesse James together with the Younger brothers. Perhaps the most famous outlaws in American history, the James-Younger gang, was formed after the Civil War and included brothers from the James and Younger families, along with various male associates and in-laws. Always armed, the gang members preferred Smith & Wesson firearms.

Source: Fly, Camillus S. *WyattEarp-andothers*. 1883. Special Media Archives Services Division, Maryland. *Wikimedia Commons*. Web. 25 Aug. 2015.

https://commons.wikimedia.org/wiki/File:WyattEarp-andothers.jpg

Figure 5.8 Photograph of Buffalo Bill Cody with rifle. Though shown carrying a rifle in this photograph, Cody also carried a Smith & Wesson pistol.

Source: Sarony. *Buffalo Bill Cody.* 1880. Sarony, New York. *Wikimedia Commons.* Web. 25 Aug. 2015.

https://commons.wikimedia.org/wiki/File:Buffalo_Bill_Cody_by_Sarony,_c1880.jpg

6 Tools for Hand and Head

Man is a weak, cowering creature when pitted against nature. His tools have been his shield and buckler and will continue to be so.

(Bealer 1976, p. 16)

The two preceding chapters have discussed the role in masculinity played by two specific kinds of tools—the motor vehicle and the gun. These tools—and their preeminent masculine brands, such as Harley-Davidson and Smith & Wesson—are those most closely linked to the expression of masculine identity in contemporary American culture. In this chapter, we will take a look at two other kinds of tools used by men. One set is literally man-ual and used for building. These are the *hand* tools; they are held in the hand and guided by the skill, muscles and eyes of the man holding them. These are the kinds of tools required for the everyday *performance* of masculinity; they are the set of objects that men are expected to have on hand and be able to use proficiently. The brands mentioned most often among those we interviewed are Craftsman, Black & Decker and John Deere. And within both these brands and the set of objects they include are two distinct types: hand tools and power tools. Craftsman, a company purchased in 1934 by Sears Roebuck Company, specializes in hand tools, although the brand now includes power tools as well.

The illustrations that follow are taken from books on early American tools (Bealer 1976) and show the types of hand tools used in both agricultural and home construction work prior to the advent of electricity and the steam engine. Men then needed both muscles and skill to plow fields, harvest grain, cut timber and plane wood, just as they needed the Winchester rifle and Colt .45 revolver to protect their households against predators and to bring home game. It is upon this basis of necessary household labor that the present day's association of men and hand tools is founded.

By the 1940s, electric and gasoline-powered tools arrived to form another sedimentary layer atop the earlier foundation of iron and wood implements—the claw hammer, the crosscut saw, the horse-drawn plow, the garden hoe, the hand drill and the axe. Now masculinity came to include competence at operating nail guns, chain saws, tractors, gasoline-propelled lawn mowers and hay balers. It required repairing or installing items such as automatic transmissions,

Figure 6.1 Photograph of hand tools on a barn wall. Hand tools such as these were vital to Colonial-era men. They were used for tasks ranging from felling trees to building furniture, houses and barns.

Source: Daderot. *Tools—Hadley Farm Museum—DSC07675.* 2013. *Wikimedia Commons.* Web. 25 Aug. 2015.

https://commons.wikimedia.org/wiki/File:Tools_-_Hadley_Farm_Museum_-_DSC07675.JPG

FIG. 1. LARGE SURFACE GRINDER

Figure 6.2 Illustration of Churchill grinding machine. Energy-powered machines such as this grinder made possible the mass production of the Industrial Revolution. Men moved from working the land to working in factories.

Source: Sitush. *American Machinist vol 38 27-Feb-1913 Churchill grinder built Pendleton built.* 2011. *Wikimedia Commons.* Web. 25 Aug. 2015.

https://commons.wikimedia.org/wiki/File:American_Machinist_vol_38_27-Feb-1913_Churchill _grinder_built_Pendleton_built.png

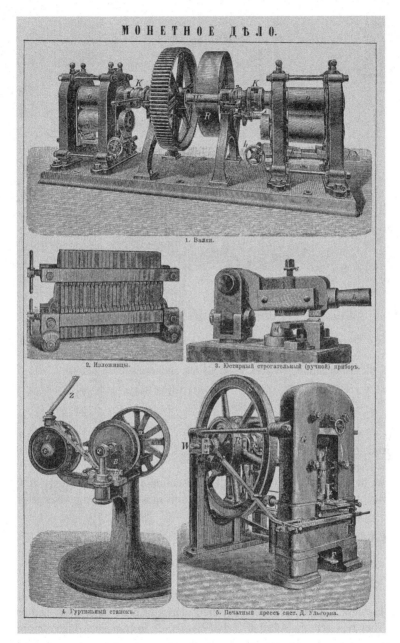

МОНЕТНОЕ ДѢЛО.

1. Валки.

2. Изложницы.

3. Юстирный строгательный (ручной) приборъ.

4. Гуртильный станокъ.

5. Печатный прессъ сист. Д. Ульгорна.

Figure 6.3 Illustrations of European machines. Wheels and belts enabled the creation of the assembly line; this acted to demasculinize factory workers by removing creativity and self-efficacy from the job. The man became a cog in the larger machine of production.

Source: Brockhaus and Efron. *Illustration from Brockhaus and Efron Encyclopedic Dictionary (1890–1907).* 1890–1907. *Wikimedia Commons.* Web. 25 Aug. 2015.

https://commons.wikimedia.org/w/index.php?title=File:Brockhaus_and_Efron_Encyclopedic_Dictionary_b38_770–0.jpg&oldid=79702608

Figure 6.4 Photograph of John Deere tractor. Perhaps the most iconic farm machine in America—the John Deere tractor. These are ubiquitous in the Appalachian Mountains, where the author currently resides. I secretly lust after one painted yellow.

Source: SF photo. *ANCASTER, ONTARIO, CANADA.* Digital Image. Shutterstock. 24 Sept 2011. Web. 03 Sept. 2015.

drywall, toilets, oil furnaces, faucets, outdoor lighting and air-conditioning units. The ante is now upped considerably.

One of the brands of tools deemed masculine across both regions of the country—John Deere—is depicted below in its most iconic form: the tractor.

And Now, the Head Tools

The men we interviewed consistently cited technologies, such as Xbox and Sony PlayStation, and digital games, such as *Call of Duty*, as representing masculinity. These constitute a dramatically different kind of tool than the manual, gasoline-motored or electrically powered modes of male labor discussed earlier. They represent the social arrival of *head tools*; instruments which require a comprehension of technology and hyperreality, as well as strategic planning and 'gaming' in virtual trials and challenges. Even though these technologies do not require physical contact with other men—or even with the world beyond one's own consciousness—they permit players to build up notoriety for excellence by quantitatively recording scores and making the comparison of these scores a field for competition. While most of the available digital venues are participated in at the individual level, in some of the games, rival teams can be put into play.

The game most often mentioned as representing masculinity is *Call of Duty*, a first-person shooter setting in which "you play most of the game looking through the eyes of the main character as he fights his way through the campaign's many scenarios" (*Call of Duty*, Black Ops II Manual, p. 1). The main character, whose eyes men are looking through, is named David Mason. He is 6′1″ and weighs 200 pounds and David is a trained counterterrorism operative and has a wide choice of weapons he can use in completing his missions.

His appearance is notable; he has about a week's growth of beard, disheveled but short dark hair, a tanned face marked by sun exposure, chest hair and camo clothing, and he carries a variety of high-performance weaponry. As such, he embodies many of the aspects of masculinity that are attractive to both men and women. He is a warrior, competent and strong; he can operate by himself in stressful, high-risk/high-danger situations; he can live off the land in rugged terrain.

Additionally, David must face violent adversaries and defeat them in order not only to protect his own life and that of his fellow warriors but also to protect America. Thus he displays both loyalty to his comrades and also the willingness to sacrifice his own life to save his country.

These are the characteristics of self-sacrifice, stoicism and courage that are among the traits most associated with masculinity.

Call of Duty players have many types of weapons to choose from; among these are machine guns, assault rifles, crossbows, rocket-propelled grenades and chemical explosives, for example C4 and Semtex.

Figure 6.5 Illustrations of automatic weapons. Combatants in online military games have several weapons to choose from. The ones shown here are all automatic and semi-automatic tactical firearms used by Special Forces units.

Source: *Set of Various Modern Weapons*. Digital Image. Shutterstock. Web. 03 Sept. 2015.

Figure 6.6 Special Forces training camp photo. This photograph depicts Special Forces training in a field setting.

Source: Ard, Michael. *Weapons Intelligence Training Course DVIDS483370*. 2011. Camo Marmal Live Fire Range, AF. *Call of Duty Black Ops and Xbox 360 Grudge Match (2)*.

https://commons.wikimedia.org/wiki/File:Weapons_Intelligence_Training_Course_DVIDS 483370.jpg

Figure 6.7 Photograph of Black Ops gamers at consoles. *Call of Duty* gamers are not 'in the field'; they are sitting in chairs operating on digital consoles.

Source: Nelson, Major. *Call of Duty Black Ops and Xbox 360 Grudge Match (2)*. 2011. Wikimedia Commons. Web. 25 Aug. 2015.

https://commons.wikimedia.org/wiki/File:Call_of_Duty_Black_Ops_and_Xbox_360_Grudge_ Match_(2).jpg

This would seem to reduce the need for strategic thinking by the combatant, but the game is structured to require increasing levels of competence and reactivity by the player. At each level of skill, new challenges appear to test the capability of the player, that is, the rules change and the player must adapt quickly and correctly or risk being wounded or killed. What is also notable about the game's environment is that enemy kills are not quick or bloodless. Melees occur frequently in which the player must literally hack hordes of oncoming terrorists to death with machetes, axes or knives or be killed in a similar fashion.

7 Alcohol and Tobacco

Johnny Walker does a great job of selling the idea of being a dignified brand; it's an excellent product; better than others. But they also go an extra mile to take care of their customers . . . For my bachelor party we are doing a Scotch tasting. I Facebook messaged them and asked if they would do it and how much it would cost. They responded: "Congratulations on your engagement; this is a big step for you in becoming a man; we will do this for free, you just pay for the venue . . . " They sell the idea that if you drink Johnny Walker, you are more of a man. I'd like to think that I don't buy into that, but I know I do. It's just a good, relaxing product and they care about their customers, which is about being a man.

(Jeff, age 29, Northeast, recently married)

There are a multitude of alcohol brands and tobacco brands named by those we interviewed as representing masculinity. Among the most commonly mentioned alcohol brands are Budweiser, Coors, Guinness, Miller, Jim Beam, Jamesons, Johnny Walker, Bud Light and Jack Daniel's. Tobacco products include Marlboro, Skoal, Copenhagen and Grizzly. The last three tobacco brands are "dip" or mouth tobacco, which is very popular among men of all ages in the Southeast. Our examination of specific brands will focus on Budweiser beer, Jack Daniel's whiskey and Jim Beam bourbon, each of which leads in its category. Marlboro's masculine imagery has already been written about *ad infinitum*, so we will take a look at Grizzly chewing tobacco (trading the iconic cowboy for a bear); Grizzly is the leading brand of smokeless tobacco.

But first, let's consider what it is about alcohol and tobacco that would make these product categories considered masculine. Beer and ale have been brewed since the fifth century BC, while whiskey was originally distilled in Europe from the 1300s onward according to the archaeological record (Damerow 2012). Tobacco was being used by Native Americans prior to the arrival of Europeans and reportedly taken back to England by Sir Walter Raleigh in the late 1500s (Damerow 2012).

Since their origination in human culture, both alcohol and tobacco have been used primarily by men (Burns 2007); thus they have a deep history of being associated with this gender. But a more imperative linkage than mere

Figure 7.1 Photograph of Clint Eastwood in western movie with cigar in mouth. Actor Clint Eastwood played tough western outlaws who almost always had cigars in their mouths.

Source: s_bukley. *Celebrity Wax Model.* Digital Image. Shutterstock. 21 July 2009. Web. 03 Sept. 2015

association is that in American culture, both alcohol and tobacco have consistently been viewed as potentially *dangerous, damaging products*, that is, they can lead to disability and death, yet the are concurrently seen as *strengthening, empowering substances*. Men smoked tobacco before going into battle during every American war from the Revolutionary War forward to Afghanistan. Western movies and television shows typically portray men at saloons drinking whiskey, smoking tobacco and gambling, with firearms dangling at their sides.

Indeed, these activities formed a constellation of admired masculine behavior for many generations of Americans. Although beer is considered manly, it is also the entry point for alcohol consumption for many; thus there is a gradation of manliness ranging from light beer to beer to dark/stout beer and ale to light-colored liquors (e.g., vodka) to the heavyweight, harsh-tasting, dark-colored 'hard' liquors such as whiskey and bourbon. The darker, the stronger, the harsher, the more masculine the alcohol is.

Both tobacco and alcohol alter men's behavior, often making it more violent, aggressive, and animalistic; that is the goal of consuming these substances for many. They can transform a man into a beast—and that may be desirable when an especially difficult foe is being faced. They permit the 'average' man to channel chaos into his psyche. Further, their consumption may help prevent cowardice; backing down from a fight, running away from the challenge—all

Figure 7.2 Photograph of western saloon. Yes, real saloons were found in the West. Note the game trophies mounted above the bar and the spittoons by the bar rail.

Source: *1897 Saloon Blackhawk.* 1897. *Wikimedia Commons.* Web. 25 Aug. 2015.

https://commons.wikimedia.org/wiki/File:1897_Saloon_Blackhawk.jpg

patently unmanly, as we have seen. As noted earlier, the behavior considered most unmasculine is not *losing* the battle but rather *running away* from it. Cowardice is the antithesis of masculinity. Alcohol and tobacco can provide the steel, the backbone, the balls necessary to stay in the fight.

Let's take a look at the most masculine brands of alcohol and tobacco.

Budweiser: The King of Beers

It's good to be king! Budweiser is the biggest selling beer in the United States and has been for eight decades. Budweiser is also the only beer brand named by virtually all of our interviewees, both male and female, as being a masculine brand. Obviously, Anheuser-Busch has done something right.

August Busch, Jr., known as Gussie, is the man who did the right thing. After taking over Anheuser-Busch from his father in the 1930s, Gussie proved to be a brilliant marketer, one who understood his customer at a core level and brilliantly put forward a set of archetypes and slogans that appealed to American men. First, he declared Budweiser to be the "king of beers." This was backed up by having a handsome, antique beer wagon drawn by a magnificent

Figure 7.3 Photograph of Jack Daniel's whiskey bottle. Jack Daniel's—the most masculine of all American whiskey brands.

Source: *Jack-daniels-hopkinsville-kentuckian-ad.* 1910. Library of Congress, Washington, D.C. *Wikimedia Commons.* Web. 25 Aug. 2015.

https://commons.wikimedia.org/wiki/File:Jack-daniels-hopkinsville-kentuckian-ad.jpg

Figure 7.4 Photograph of Budweiser Clydesdales and beer wagon. The Budweiser Clydesdales are iconic masculine symbols.

Source: Alexanderphoto7. *Budweiser Clydesdales*. Digital Image. Shutterstock. 4 July 2013. Web. 03 Sept. 2015.

team of eight Clydesdale draft horses serve as the iconic image associated with the brand. The Clydesdales and the heavy, ornate wagon were first used in April 7, 1933, to celebrate the repeal of Prohibition; they continue to signify the company, making many appearances a year to promote the brand . The horses themselves are huge, powerful, muscular and handsome—extremely appropriate male symbols. They even performed as athletes, winning pulling contests at state fairs and equestrian events during the 1930s to the 1960s.

Gussie understood the allure that athletics had for American men. In 1953, he was one of the first businessmen to buy a professional sports franchise, the St. Louis Cardinals, building the team a stadium and exclusively selling Anheuser-Busch beers to the fans. The Cardinals' radio announcers, Harry Caray and Jack Buck, also served as spokespersons for Budweiser, as did members of the Cardinals baseball club.

Anheuser-Busch now ranks as the leading advertiser in sports marketing. I was stunned when I saw the roster of their sponsorships. It includes Major League Baseball, the NBA, the NFL, the PGA, the Kentucky Derby, the UFC, NASCAR, Daytona Speedway, the National Hot Rod Association, National Shooting Sports Foundation, the FIFA World Cup, USA Snowboarding and Skiing, the 2008 Olympic Games and the NHL. Recalling that several of these activities are the ones named by those we interviewed as being masculine, one can see that Budweiser saturates men where they play.

August Busch III, who displaced his father in 1975 as president of Anheuser-Busch, was a similarly brilliant marketer to men. Budweiser's advertising campaigns have used a series of anthropomorphized objects and animals to represent not only the beer but the male beer drinker.

Consider the Bud Bowl, which appeared on the Super Bowl between 1989 and 1996 (Cancelada 2008). Here the animated beer bottles represent men battling to make it into the end zone and score. Then there is the pugnacious and macho Spuds McKenzie, a bull terrier, who served to signify Budweiser and its drinkers—as a 'party animal'—from 1987 to 1992 (Holleman 2008). In 1995, Budweiser brought out Johnny—a prototypical beer-drinking 'everyman' who claims to bond with his male companion, but really wants to sponge a beer. His companion, who brought the Budweiser to the fishing trip, hunting trip, ball game and so forth, recognizes this ruse and refuses to share. This was followed by additional renderings of men as animals—the Budweiser Frogs, the Budweiser Lizards—and by groups of men just being men, as in the "Whassup" series and the "Dude" series.

What is consistent across these is a sense of masculine humor. Guys like to be gross, they can see themselves as animals, they enjoy hanging out and ribbing each other. Budweiser, more than any other beer, has grasped the essence of masculine camaraderie and put it into a variety of memorable and amusing forms.

Jack Daniel's

In researching this brand, I discovered that some male consumers of Jack Daniel's were surprised to learn that the eponymous man actually existed. He did. The images of Jack shown in the advertising, the town of Lynchburg, Tennessee, the Hollow in which the water for the whiskey is obtained and the old store in which it was first sold (and which now serves as a part of the distillery tour) are all genuine. This—and its origin as an illegal liquor, or moonshine—serve as the root of its appeal for many men.

Jack Daniel was the small, poor son of a farmer living in rural Middle Tennessee. He was born in 1849; his mother died soon thereafter. Jack came of age during the Civil War. The family's farm was ravaged during the war, and his father never recovered financially or emotionally from the loss. The family was of Scotch-Irish descent and accustomed to turning a portion of its annual corn crop into whiskey (Hirschman, Brown and Maclaran 2006).

When his father died, Jack became apprenticed to his uncle, Dan Call, with whom he began distilling whiskey for sale. Together they operated a 'pot still' that made whiskey in 8-gallon batches. The resulting moonshine, so named because it was manufactured illegally without a license or payment of taxes to the federal government (an institution deeply resented by these Southerners), was put into homemade earthenware jugs. Jack loaded it onto a mule-drawn wagon and sold it in nearby towns and villages. The whiskey Jack and his uncle produced was superior in quality to that distilled by other local 'shiners, because they used a sour mash process; this removed much of the sugar from the liquor, giving it a more mellow, nuanced flavor with less of a hangover after consumption.

As the quality of their whiskey became more widely known, Jack would drive his team of mules as far as Huntsville, Alabama, where the market was bigger and the prices higher. As Krass (2004) notes, making this journey as a small 16-year-old was a brave—bordering on reckless—undertaking. But Jack was a true entrepreneur; he had come from nothing and likely felt that 'making it' was worth the risk. By 1875, Jack Daniel had become the sole proprietor of the distilling operation.

While the business was profitable, it lacked a distinctive identity. Jack arrived at the name Old Number 7 and chose to use a square glass bottle with a black label to make his brand stand out from others in the area. He relocated his production facility to a ravine next to a limestone cliff on the outskirts of Lynchburg, Tennessee. The cold, limestone-filtered water coming from a spring in the cave below the cliff was ideal for making sour mash whiskey, and the Jack Daniel's brand was now fully born.

After winning the gold medal at the St. Louis World's Fair, Jack's brand became widely recognized as an excellent, handcrafted whiskey. It was favored by cognoscenti politicians such as John Nance Garner, Harry Truman, J. Edgar Hoover and Winston Churchill.

But it was an article in *Fortune* magazine in 1951 that popularized the brand to a national audience. The article described the Jack Daniel's brand as "rare, romantic and utterly masculine"; the liquor preferred by the genuinely powerful—a secret indulgence shared by the movers and shakers in business and politics. Five years later, the Brown-Forman Distilling Company purchased the Jack Daniel's brand and polished this positioning with an advertising campaign that has remained effective for the past six decades. The campaign focuses on the history of the brand and most significantly the *lifestyle* of the men who make it. Typically they are shown telling stories around a wood stove, whittling on the front porch of the original distillery building, grooming the mule team, loading wood into pickup trucks and tending the sour mash kettles.

The wonderful beauty of this is that it recalls the masculinity of traditional rural life—when men worked with their hands, took time off to josh with one another, wore comfortable clothes to work and performed their chosen tasks with skill and devotion. It was a time when individual crafts*man*ship and work*man*ship were appreciated and valued in and of themselves. Each individual man has an important role to play in creating the final product. Each man has pride in his day's work and yet also has time to enjoy the company of other men.

Life in such a setting is more genuine; people's lives and work are interwoven in ways that are both subtle and satisfying. Such men's lives are lived in the present and not in a constant frantic pursuit of the future. This is likely a world that many contemporary men find preferable—at least from time to time—to the overplanned, tightly scheduled, frenetic, structured existence they now lead. And this is why Jack Daniel's is the top-selling American whiskey in the world.

Grizzly Tobacco

Every can and pouch of Grizzly tobacco has a huge, angry grizzly bear on the front. This iconic masculine symbol promises to give the user strength, power and aggressiveness. And it does. Grizzly delivers more nicotine to the user's bloodstream than any other tobacco product, and it does so in a matter of seconds. Because it contains nicotine and is addictive, Grizzly is prohibited from advertising its brand on television, and its print ads and in-store signing must carry large black-box warnings stating that it is not a safe alternative to cigarettes.

Grizzly was introduced to the marketplace in 2001 as an alternative to cigarettes (public smoking bans were becoming widespread at that time) and quickly became the best selling 'smokeless tobacco,' garnering a 25 percent market share. Grizzly is owned by the American Snuff Corporation (Louisville, Kentucky), along with several other smokeless tobacco brands mentioned by our interviewees (e.g., Skoal, Copenhagen), but it is more clearly directed toward its target market than these foreign-sounding brands. That target market consists of rural males, especially in the Southeast, who enjoy the outdoors, go hunting and fishing, drive pickup trucks, drink Budweiser and Jack Daniel's and likely wear Nike sneakers when they are not wearing their hunting boots.

In support of this analysis is an advertisement that appears in the August 2013 issue of *Hunting Magazine*. The headline reads, "You may Never Go Indoors Again" and presents the details of the Grizzly Man Cave Give-Away: Outdoor Edition. This promotion offers a $50,000 grand prize and can only be entered by visiting the Grizzly.com website (a legal requirement for all tobacco products). Among the prizes are an aluminum fishing boat complete with motor and trailer, a barbecue grill shaped like a .45-caliber gun, a John Deere camouflage-colored ATV and a camping trailer—masculinity heaven!

Clearly what the reader should be cognizant of at this point is that there is a protomasculine lifestyle that is shared (at least in fantasy) by many within this gendered subculture. Grizzly tobacco did not gain its market share through conventional advertising media; it did so through patterns of shared male experiences, 'word of mouth' (pun intended) and observation of admired others. Within the armed forces units stationed in Iraq and Afghanistan use of smokeless tobacco, and especially Grizzly brand, is estimated to be as high as 50 percent.

This ties in to the discussion at the beginning of the chapter, which notes that intoxicants (e.g., alcohol) and stimulants (e.g., nicotine) are historically used across cultures by males engaging in combat. These substances heighten aggression and dull pain; thus they contribute to the warrior's effectiveness, especially in hand-to-hand combat.

8 Masculine Grooming and Apparel

Clean shirt, new shoes, and I don't know where I'm goin' to.
Silk shirt, black tie, I don't need a reason why.
They come a runnin' just as fast as they can.
'Cause every girl crazy for a sharp-dressed man.

("Sharp-Dressed Man," ZZ Top, 1983)

In this chapter, we take a look at the histories of four personal-appearance brands that are consistently named as representing masculinity. Three are grooming products—Old Spice, Axe and Gillette—while one is an apparel brand—Nike. I am grouping together Old Spice and Axe because of both the similarity of their product lines and the similarity of their strategies for communicating masculinity. Gillette and Nike will be discussed together because they have very successfully used virtually identical branding strategies.

Old Spice was introduced in 1938 by Procter & Gamble and had the enormous advantage of creating the product category of men's toiletries virtually without competition. The original iconography was of an older ship captain who steered the vessel. This brought to mind the ruggedness of the sea and its effects on men's skin, especially the irritation of shaving. The Old Spice scent is reminiscent of the original spice trading sea ventures, as well as linking to the New England whaling tradition. Early advertising showed the logo Old Spice trading ship and one or two captains in full dress uniform.

This set of images provided a sense of tradition, adventure and manliness that grounded the brand as conservatively masculine. However, by the sixties, several new men's fragrance toiletries had entered the market and were targeted toward younger men. Brands such as Canoe, English Leather and Drakkar Noir replaced Old Spice for the younger generation of men by appealing to sexuality. Old Spice fought back with a series of ads directed toward young men featuring waif-like young women. In one example, the headline reads, "Lea has a soft spot for guys who wear Old Spice"; the pretty blonde woman wears a white, loose dress but has her arms around a large tree trunk—suggesting both a strong man and a large penis.

Toward the end of the sixties, Old Spice introduced a new fragrance, Old Spice Burley, to compete for the younger male market. The headline in these advertisements emphasizes being manly, and the color scheme is darker—the Burley bottle, itself, is black with a white Old Spice ship. By the 1970s, Old Spice had introduced a musk-scented version to compete with the many musk-based men's toiletry brands on the market. The brand seemed to be playing catch-up and was lagging in its knowledge of the market. The advertising for this campaign is more directly sexual, suggesting that wearing the scent would be "very convincing" to a woman.

During the new millennium, Old Spice revved up the volume in several ways, succeeding in breaking away from the pack of men's toiletry brands and reestablishing itself as the category archetype. The most recent headline, "Smell like a man, man," stakes out the central claim to masculinity: all other scents are cast as less manly. The new strategy included using aggressive, athletic men such as NASCAR driver Tony Stewart as endorsers.

Print ads during this time period were explicitly sexual and meant to compete with Axe for the young men's market. A 2007 Old Spice Body Spray trucker ad shows a hot 'country girl' talking on the CB radio while flanked by two phallic metal diesels. The 2008 centaur in the shower advertisement shows a white man/black horse centaur and carries the headline: "It's got two things," referencing not only the two attributes of the Old Spice body wash but also the fact that the showering centaur has two sets of genitals. This of course is a wonderful foreshadowing of the 2010 "Smell like a man, man" campaign featuring Isaiah Mustafa, a black man, astride a white horse. The incorporation of logo lines such as Danger Zone and The Scent of Courage have also helped to increase the testosterone level of Old Spice.

Axe

During the last decade, the only men's toiletry brand giving Old Spice a run for its money in terms of masculinity ranking is Axe. Axe was first introduced in early 2001 by Unilever and is targeted toward 14- to 25-year-old males. Although the Axe advertising campaign has been criticized by women's groups as sexist and encouraging of inappropriate behavior toward women, it has been enormously successful in attracting its intended audience. Men in the younger age group, as learned from our research, see masculinity as heavily tilted toward sexual prowess. Virtually all the younger men we interviewed report that "having sex" and "chasing women" are key masculine activities. Between the ages of 17 and 27, most men are not focused on masculine activities that require commitment, responsibility or self-denial. Those orientations come later, especially after marriage and children.

Younger men want very much to prove themselves as masculine. They engage in competitions of physical strength and power against other men; they use athletic prowess to become champions and leaders; they pursue young women to prove to themselves and to others that they are potent and hetero-sexual. Much of this age group's activities are spent in testing, questing and proving. Their masculine identities are under construction, not yet formed, so it becomes vital for them to pursue recognition through competition and con-quest. Young men who avoid competition or fail at this stage are often socially bullied and demeaned.

Thus the Axe brand promises surefire victory in the sexual conquest arena: Wear me and she will jump into bed with you. Splash on some of this, and women will grab you on the street.

Fear of rejection is abated. I *will* score!

Gillette

And now, onward to facial hair. One of the most fascinating characteristics of men, from a woman's perspective, is that they grow hair on their faces. Every day. Truly this is a strange affliction. From a man's perspective, the growth of facial hair must also seem undesirable and tedious at times. Yet it is also a signal of manhood and sexual maturity. Boys become men when their bodies grow hair—most noticeably on their faces. The history of shaving indicates that facial hair has been viewed both positively and negatively as a male fash-ion accessory. In American Indian culture, for instance, facial hair was sparse, and what did grow was considered unattractive; thus it was plucked out. In several Arab cultures, men are expected to grow a mustache to signal their masculinity and sexual prowess. Orthodox Jewish men are expected to grow their beards as long as possible as a sign of devotion to the Torah.

Both Alexander the Great and Julius Caesar were clean shaven, which may have contributed to the preference for clean-shaven faces among men in West-ern Europe. (It also apparently was more advantageous in hand-to-hand combat to not have facial hair that could be grabbed by an adversary.)

Being clean shaven in contemporary American society marks one as a pro-fessional man but also as a conformist—and hence, less masculine than, say, a ponytailed, stubble-faced construction worker or perhaps most emphatically a long-haired, full-bearded Hell's Angel on a Harley.

Currently, women's fashion advertising features male models with muscular bodies and stubble-covered faces. To women, this suggests a guy who will not only be great in bed but also not likely to jump out of that bed, don a suit and rush off to work the next morning. (On the other hand, women also hypocriti-cally want a guy who has a lot of money, so maybe we are all searching for an entrepreneur hunk who looks great, does not have to keep a tight schedule and can afford lots of stuff.)

Into this medley of meanings and signifiers comes Gillette—"the best a man can get."

In my view, Gillette made itself into the most-mentioned masculine brand of shaving equipment not by focusing on shaving *per se* but rather by linking itself to *masculine men who shave*. As will be documented, Gillette was the

Figure 8.1 Marble bust of Alexander the Great. As this marble bust shows, Alexander the Great was not only clean shaven but also extraordinarily handsome.

Source: Pedersen, Gunnar Bach. *Aleksander-d-store.* 2006. *Wikimedia Commons.* Web. 25 Aug. 2015.

https://commons.wikimedia.org/wiki/File:Aleksander-d-store.jpg

first major American corporation to pair itself with professional athletes. In so doing, it carved a path that Nike, whom we will discuss subsequently, also followed to category dominance.

In 1939, at the end of the Great Depression and just prior to World War II, Gillette became the primary sponsor of the World Series, then broadcast

Figure 8.2 Marble bust of Julius Caesar. Julius Caesar, iconic emperor and world conqueror, was clean shaven.

Source: *Caesar. Wikimedia Commons.* Web. 25 Aug. 2015.

https://commons.wikimedia.org/wiki/File:Caesar.jpg

Figure 8.3 Photograph of Hell's Angels on Harleys. Here comes trouble: Hell's Angels, Harleys, helmets and facial hair!

Source: *uncleru. Oslo. Protest of motorcycle clubs.* Digital Image. Shutterstock. 14 Sept 2013. Web. 03 Sept. 2015.

Figure 8.4 Photograph of handsome male model. Nice!

Source: *Confident young man*. Digital Image. Shutterstock. Web. 03 Sept. 2015.

on radio. Red Barber and Bob Elson, the two announcers for the series, gave sales pitches for Gillette razors over the course of the series that were perhaps even more successful than the actual pitchers in the game—by the end of the series, more than 2.5 million Gillette World Series Specials had been sold (McKibben 1998).

Gillette recognized that it had tapped into a deep emotional linkage between regular men and the professional athletes they admire. In 1940, Gillette became the official sponsor of the Orange Bowl, Sugar Bowl, Cotton Bowl and Rose Bowl, as well as the Kentucky Derby.

Creating an even stronger masculine linkage was Gillette's next promotional move, which was to sponsor the Friday Night Fights—soon expanded to other days—first on radio and then on television. Here were individual men engaged in physical combat with only one declared the victor—this was masculinity at its most primitive and compelling. The entire package of Gillette-sponsored athletic events became labeled Gillette's Cavalcade of Sports and continued into the 1950s.

Concurrently, Gillette became the designated supplier of shaving equipment for the US military services during World War II. When these men returned home, they were accustomed to Gillette equipment and, as heroic soldiers and warriors, they carried a cachet of masculinity that radiated in civilian life. Gillette was the *man's* razor. In 1955, during the World Series, Gillette introduced its "Look sharp, feel sharp" jingle with the mnemonic bell ringing at the end of each line. Iconic athletes such as Willie Mays and Whitey Ford served as spokesmen for Gillette—a pattern that Gillette continued with other prominent athletes through the 1960s and 1970s.

In essence, the concept of "I want to be like Mike [Michael Jordan]," which Nike rode to remarkable success, is a direct descendant of the "I want to be like Willie" and "I want to be like Whitey," which Gillette invented three decades earlier. By the 1970s, Gillette had broadened its masculine models to include actors who embodied the concept.

In the late 1980s, Gillette introduced the "Best a man can get" theme, which debuted during the 1989 Super Bowl. It is a superb encapsulation of its image and appeal from the 1940s forward—linked to the archetypal male sporting event and announcing superiority over all other brands. What man would want to shave with something less than the best?

Nike

Likely everyone reading this book (mostly men, I assume) knows the story of Nike's partnership with Wieden + Kennedy and their 'discovery' of rookie Michael Jordan and the extraordinary success of the "Just do it" campaign. This gives us the 'who' and 'how' aspects of Nike's success story, but it does not give us the 'why' of its perceived masculinity. Nike is the only apparel brand named by our cross-section of men as representing masculinity; other brands, such as Adidas, Calvin Klein, Hugo Boss and Men's Wearhouse, are also mentioned by many of those to whom we talked, but only Nike was consistently cited across age groups and regions. Why?

In my view, the special relationship Nike has formed over the decade with men derives from the perception that the company sees itself as striving continuously to improve its performance and to prove its own worth. American men see themselves in the same terms. There is never a final moment of 'being a man' that is sufficient. One can never rest on one's laurels. There is always a mountain unclimbed, a race not yet run, a challenge not yet undertaken. The game is not over until you are dead. And then you have left a son behind who will continue the legacy of manhood. As early as 1977, Nike had put forward the tagline "There is no finish line."

Being a man never becomes a 'given' in one's life; it is always subject to test, always an attribute that is under construction. Men fear that one day, they will fail to act in a masculine way. A challenge will come along that they will avoid. It is this possibility of potential loss of masculinity that drives them forward to always do their best, even if that best is not always sufficient to win the competition.

One late-career commercial with Michael Jordan communicates this idea and ideal perfectly:

> The commercial shows Jordan walking through a room and you can hear him talking about the pitfalls he has suffered on the court . . . He mentions missing more than 9,000 shots over his career and failing after being trusted by his teammates 26 times to make the game-winning shot. . . . Jordan exits through a door as you hear his final statement, "I've failed over and over in my life, and that's why I succeed."
>
> (Carbasho 2010, p. 4)

One need not fear failure, only not trying. Thus, the "Just do it" theme resonates with every man.

Because Nike manufactures shoes and athletic apparel, which are *worn* by the purchaser, the company has the opportunity to serve a magical function as well. There are many, many heroic myths that include instances of warriors putting on special capes, coats, boots or helmets that give them superhuman powers or protect them from harm. By putting on a pair of Nike Jordan basketball shoes or wearing a Manning football jersey, the man or boy inside feels capable of doing what the eponymous athlete can do. He is *transformed*—he can leap, run, hit, catch the ball, clear the hurdle with the same skill as the athlete whose name he wears.

He is not only *like* Mike; he *is* Mike.

9 Retail Masculinity or the In-Store Man Cave

Our final chapter takes a look at three retail manifestations of the 'man cave'; three stores were consistently named by the men to whom we talked as masculine preserves. What is especially notable about them is that they are not brands, per se—recall that we specifically asked for masculine brands from our informants. But these three stores were named none-the-less as brands that represent masculinity. They are Outdoor World/Bass Pro Shops, Dick's Sporting Goods and Men's Wearhouse. The first two stores are places where sporting equipment and sports apparel can be purchased; the third is a retail store devoted entirely to men's dress and casual apparel. In all three cases, they have been successful in creating spaces where 'men can be men,' where men feel they are in a masculine environment. And indeed when I, a female, visited each one to check it out more closely, it was primarily populated by men, both as sales personnel and customers.

Let's start with Outdoor World/Bass Pro Shops. The store I visited is located in Charlotte, North Carolina, in a mall, Concord Mills, that has both regular retail stores and a wide selection of off-price retailers, for example T. J. Maxx. The Bass Pro Shops store is one of the large anchor units and is enormous—more than 130,000 square feet on two levels. The entrance to the store is festooned with the heads of stuffed game animals and plaques commemorating the hunter or fisherman who bagged them. There is a large bulletin board called the Braggin' Board, with snapshots of area residents who are displaying their trophy animals and fish. Upon entering the store, to the immediate right is a shooting range with 'pop-guns' children can use to shoot a variety of pretend game animals set up as targets. A taxidermy black bear, some whitetail deer, bobcats, wild geese, wild turkeys and pheasants are set near the shooting range.

To the immediate left is a restaurant, Uncle Buck's, which serves down-home food such as cheeseburgers, french fries, grits, apple pie, barbeque ribs, fried catfish, pork sandwiches and sodas. The enormous square footage of the store, itself, is decorated to resemble a wooded glen with cedar timbers and tree trunks located throughout the lower level. Merchandising displays are devoted to a mixture of outdoor equipment, primarily hunting and fishing, as well as apparel for these sports. Tents are set up along with propane camping stoves and camp furniture to resemble outdoor campsites. Tree stands for deer hunting are displayed on artificial tree trunks.

Figure 9.1 Photograph of Bass Pro Shops exterior. Welcome to the real man cave! Bass Pro Shops has it all—guns, ammo, hunting gear, fishing gear, trophy animals, tents, sleeping bags, knives and lots and lots of wood beams.

Source: EMcCutchan. *Bass Pro Shops entrance.* 2005. Springfield, Missouri. *Wikimedia Commons.* Web. 25 Aug. 2015.

https://commons.wikimedia.org/wiki/File:Bass_Pro_Shops_entrance.JPG

The store also features an enormous two-story aquarium filled with very large (trophy-size and beyond) game fish. Fishing tackle and boats are set up inside the store so that their utility can be checked out by customers. Perhaps most notably, there is a remarkable collection of shooting weapons ranging from simple handguns to semiautomatic tactical rifles. The store offers shooting lessons for beginners and advanced firearms users. Racks and racks of camouflage gear are available for different hunting climates.

There are GPS tracking devices, thermal underwear, emergency medical kits, knives for hand-to-hand combat and dressing game, fishing lures, nets and gaffing hooks, rods, reels, canoes and kayaks, emergency flares, compasses and digital mapping devices. There are hammocks, mosquito netting and spray, snakebite antivenin, hiking boots, waist-high waders, fly-tying feathers, sleeping bags suitable for subzero conditions and mountain climbing/rappelling line and hooks. There are ready-to-eat meals and water-purifying tablets. One gets the feeling that if Armageddon did strike Charlotte, both the doomsday preppers and the *Duck Dynasty* family—along with all red-blooded American males within a hundred-mile radius—would be headed for Bass Pro Shops.

Figure 9.2 Photograph of Bass Pro Shops interior rifle display. Yes, this is the place you can get all the tactical, black ops weaponry you need for the coming Armageddon.

Source: Cop, Fish. *Lodge007*. 2005. *Wikimedia Commons*. Web. 25 Aug. 2015.

https://commons.wikimedia.org/wiki/File:Lodge007.JPG

Some background on the history of Bass Pro Shops is helpful to understanding its 'good-ol-boy' masculine mystique. The retail enterprise evolved out of a bait-and-tackle shop at the back of a liquor store near Branson, Missouri, in 1972. By 1975, the bait shop had grown into the world's largest mail-order sporting goods store, carrying lines of outdoors equipment for fishing, hunting and camping. This led to the development of store labels devoted to the rural pursuits of hunting and fishing, for example, American Rod and Gun offerings and Bass Tracker boats and trailer packages.

Perhaps not surprisingly—given its old-time form of masculinity—Bass Pro Shops is closely linked to both the National Rifle Association (NRA) and NASCAR. In 2013, the NRA opened its national firearms museum next to the flagship (300,000 sq.-ft.) Bass Pro Shops store in Springfield, Missouri. According to the publicity material, "The museum will host firearms and artwork from the Remington Arms Company factory collection, a multi-million dollar collection of US Military sidearms, engraved Colt revolvers of the American frontier and firearms of US Presidents Teddy Roosevelt and Dwight Eisenhower." These names should sound familiar to readers, as they have appeared in earlier chapters. Similarly, the sponsorship affiliation of Bass Pro

Figure 9.3 Photograph of NASCAR driver Martin Truex Jr. in his Bass Pro Shops–sponsored car.

Source: Daredevil, Freewheeling. *Martin Truex, Jr. 2008 Bass Pro Shops Chevy Impala.* 2008. *Wikimedia Commons.* Web. 25 Aug. 2015.

https://commons.wikimedia.org/wiki/File:Martin_Truex,_Jr._2008_Bass_Pro_Shops_Chevy_Impala.jpg

Shops with NASCAR drivers such as Dale Earnhardt, Tony Stewart and Martin Truex Jr. resonates with the traditional masculine pastime of stock car racing. Clearly, there is a cultural coherence of masculine markers that is recognized by this very successful marketer.

While Bass Pro Shops does carry team sports equipment, it is primarily targeted toward the outdoorsman—the man who is comfortable traversing through nature, whether hiking, camping, hunting or fishing. By contrast, Dick's Sporting Goods is directed toward the man who plays team or individual competitive sports. The footwear here, for example, features various brands of track shoes, basketball shoes, baseball shoes, soccer shoes and football shoes, together with jerseys from pro football, hockey, basketball and baseball teams. There are large displays of basketballs, footballs and soccer balls together with lacrosse sticks. Notably, there are also several brands of golf and tennis equipment and shoes, suggesting that Dick's represents perhaps a more 'upscale' variety of masculinity than Bass Pro Shops. Supporting this interpretation is their merchandising of 'fashion' brands of sports apparel, such as Hurley, Volcom, Puma and Patagonia, which skew toward a younger, more professional type of male customer.

Dick's also directs its appeal to indoor training activities, featuring a broad selection of exercise/gym equipment, such as Bowflex, weights, treadmills, which are for the individual male who wants to build up his physique. There is also a section of the store devoted to sports fans that features large photos of professional sports teams and celebrity sports players. Star player name jerseys are available, as is autographed memorabilia.

Dick's Sporting Goods has a backstory with both similarities and differences to that of Bass Pro Shops. Dick's is similar in that it started as a small bait-and-tackle shop in Binghamton, New York. However, unlike Bass Pro Shops, which is still managed by its founding entrepreneur, Tom Morris (the son of the Dick's original founder) greatly increased expansion of the store throughout the Northeast during the 1990s. Dick's marketing program also serves as a point of differentiation for its masculine appeal, being much more oriented toward sponsorship of professional sporting events through ESPN, especially football, soccer, golf and running. These are not outdoorsy activities and are removed from the 'nature' aspect of traditional masculinity.

Men's Wearhouse

The raison d'etre of Men's Wearhouse can be summed up in a simple phrase: It is a retail store where men assist other men in dressing like men. The essence of its masculinity is that it is an all-male hangout where the important but often excruciatingly awkward task of choosing men's apparel is simplified and made safe. The stores are decorated in neutral, masculine colors; the staff is all male (and conservatively dressed and appears to be entirely heterosexual). It is masculine, because it makes men feel *empowered about their appearance*, especially in professional or formal settings.

Significantly, choosing professional apparel is one of the aspects of men's lives about which they feel least confident and most vulnerable to failure. What if they pair items that are unflattering? What if the clothes fit poorly? What if the suit is out of style? What if the tie and shirt do not match? Face is lost and masculinity suffers—in front of other men. Men's Wearhouse creatively solves this by providing an apparel selection, staff and tailoring services that ensure the male customer walks out with matching pieces that fit well, are color coordinated and are currently in style. As the former (now fired) company founder and CEO, George Zimmer, put it in the highly successful advertising campaign, "You're gonna look good. I guarantee it."

What the store chain understands implicitly—and communicates explicitly— is that a man's business suit is his armor. It is what he goes into battle with every workday; it is what he hopes will get his overtures to attractive women successfully received. The right clothes can make the man—and they can ensure he will be perceived as successful, as desirable, as dominant.

Bibliography

Andersson, M. (1994), *Sexual Selection*, Princeton: Princeton University Press.

Baker, Donna (1999), *Vintage Anheuser-Busch*, Atglen, PA: Schiffer Books.

Batra, Rajiv, Aaron Ahuvia and Richard P. Bagozzi (2012), "Brand Love," *Journal of Marketing*, 76 (March), 1–16.

Bealer, Alex W. (1976), *The Tools that Built America*, Mineola, NY: Dover Publications.

Belk, Russell W. (1988), "Possessions and the Extended Self," *Journal of Consumer Research*, 15 (2), 139–168.

Birks, Melanie and Jane Mills (2011), *Grounded Theory: A Practical Guide*, Los Angeles: Sage.

Boorman, Dean K. (2002), *The History of Smith & Wesson Firearms*, Guilford, CT: Lyons Press.

Boudreau, Brenda (2011), "Sexually suspect: masculine anxiety in the films of Neil LaBute" in E. Watson and M. Shaw (eds.) *Performing American Masculinities: The 21st Century Man in Popular Literature*, pp. 35–57. Bloomington, IN: Indiana University Press.

Bowen, G. A. (2008), "Naturalistic Inquiry and the Saturation Concept," *Qualitative Research*, 8 (1), 137–152.

Bowling, Brad (2010), *Ford Mustang*, Minneapolis, Minn.: Motor Books—MBI Publishing.

Budweiser (2011), *Calendar*, Indianapolis, IN: TF Publishing.

Buerkle, C. Wesley (2011), "Masters of Their Domain" in Watson and Shaw, pp. 9–37.

Burns, Eric (2007), *The Smoke of the Gods: A Social History of Tobacco*, Philadelphia: Temple University Press.

Buss, David M. (1994), *The Evolution of Desire*, New York: Basic Books.

Cancelada, Greg (2008), "The Early Days: Recognition of Innovation", in Bob Rose and Jean Buchanan (eds.), *Anheuser-Busch: The King's Reign*, St. Louis, St. Louis Dispatch Books, pp. 46–59.

Carbasho, Tracy (2010), *Nike*, Santa Barbara, CA: Greenwood Press.

Cawelti, John (1984), *The Six-Gun Mystique*, Bowling Green, OH: Bowling Green University Popular Press.

Chapman, R. (1988), "The Great Pretender: Variations on the New Man Theme," in R. Chapman and J. Rutherford (eds.), *Male Order: Unwrapping Masculinity*, London: Lawrence and Wishart, pp. 245–48.

Charmaz, K. (2006), *Constructing Grounded Theory*, London: Sage.

Clint Eastwood (1983), Dialogue by actor Clint Eastwood in the film "Sudden Impact", Released by Warner Brothers Pictures.

Connell, R. W. (2005), *Masculinities*, Berkeley: University of California Press.

Corbin, Juliet and Anselm Strauss (2008), *Basics of Qualitative Research,* Third Edition, Los Angeles, CS: Sage Publications.

Damerow, Peter (2012), "Sumerian Beer: The Origins off Brewing Technology in Ancient Mesopotamia", *Cunieform Digital Library Journal,* Volume 22, January.

De Grazia, Victoria (1996), *The Sex of Things: Gender and Consumption in Historical Perspective,* Berkeley: University of California Press.

Desai, Kalpesh Kaushik and Kevin Lane Keller (2002), "The Effects of Ingredient Branding Strategies on Host Brand Extendability," *Journal of Marketing,* 66 (1), 73–93.

Diamond, Nina, John F. Sherry, Jr., Albert M. Muñiz, Jr., Mary Ann McGrath, Robert V. Kozinets, and Stephania Borghini (2009), "American Girl and the Brand Gestalt: Closing the Loop on Sociocultural Branding Research," *Journal of Marketing,* 73 (3), 118–134.

Earnest, Brian (2010), *Mustang: The Original Pony Car,* Iola, WI: Krause Publications.

Edwards, T. (2006), *Cultures of Masculinity,* London: Routledge.

Faludi, Susan (1999), *Stiffed: The Betrayal of the American Man,* New York: HarperCollins.

Folstad, I. and A. J. Karter (1992), "Parasites, Bright Males, and the Immunocompetence Handicap," *American Naturalist,* 139, 603–622.

Ford Motor Company (2013), *Introducing the New 2013 F-150,* Dealer brochure.

Forty, Adrian (1986), *Objects of Desire: Design and Society from Wedgwood to IBM,* New York: Pantheon.

Friend, Craig T. (2009), *Southern Masculinity,* Athens: University of Georgia Press.

Geary, D. C. and M. V. Flinn (2001), "Evolution of Human Parental Behavior," *Parenting: Science and Practice,* 1, 5–61.

Geary, David C., Jacob Virgil and Jennifer Byrd-Craven (2003), Evolution of Human Mate Choice, web.missouri.edu.

Geary, David C., Jacob Virgil and Jennifer Byrd-Craven (2004), "Evolution of Human Mate Choice," *Journal of Sex Research,* 41 (1), 27–42.

Glaser, B. G. (1978), *Theoretical Sensitivity,* Mill Valley, CAS: Sociological Press.

Hamilton, W. D. and M. Zuk (1982, October 22), "Heritable True Fitness and Bright Birds: A Role for Parasites," *Science,* 218, 384–387.

Harley-Davidson Reader (2006), *Motorbooks,* Minneapolis, MN: MBI Publishing.

Henderson & Co., P. (2002), *Turn-of-the-Century Farm Tools and Implements,* New York: Dover Publishing.

Henshaw, Thomas (editor) (1993), *The History of Winchester Firearms 1866–1992,* Clinton, NJ: Winchester Press.

Hirschman, Elizabeth C. (2003), "Men, Dogs, Guns and Cars: The Semiotics of Rugged Individualism," *Journal of Advertising,* 32 (1, Spring), 9–22.

Hirschman, Elizabeth C., Stephen Brown and Pauline Maclaran (2006), *Two Continents, One Culture,* Johnson City, TN: Overmountain Press.

Holleman, Joe (2008), "Advertising Spotted Dogs, Talking Frogs", in Bob Rose and Jean Buchanan (eds.), *Anheuser-Busch: The King's Reign,* St. Louis, St. Louis Dispatch Books, pp. 122–131.

Holt, Douglas and Craig J. Thompson (2004), "Man-of-Action Heroes: The Pursuit of Heroic Masculinity in Everyday Consumption," *Journal of Consumer Research,* 31 (September), 425–449.

Holt, Douglas B. and Craig J. Thompson (2005), "Man of Action Heroes: The Pursuit of Heroic Masculinity", *Journal of Consumer Research,* 13 (2), 425–440.

Honey, Maureen (1984), *Creating Rosie the Riveter: Class, Gender, and Propaganda During World War II*, Amherst: University of Massachusetts Press.

Irons, W. (1983), "Human Female Reproductive Strategies," in S. Wasser and M. Waterhouse (eds.), *Social Behavior of Female Vertebrates,* New York: Academic Press, 169–213.

Jinks, Roy G. and Sandra C. Klein (2006), *Smith and Wesson*, Charleston, SC: Arcadia Publishing.

Keller, Kevin Lane (2009), "Building Strong Brands in a Modern Marketing Communications Environment," *Journal of Marketing Communications*, 15 (2), 139–155.

Kimmel, Michael (1996, 2012), *Manhood in America: A Cultural History*, Oxford: Oxford University Press.

Kimmel, M., J. Hearn, and R. W. Connell (2004), *Handbook of Research on Men and Masculinities,* Thousand Oaks, CA: Sage Publications.

Kirkham, Pat (1996), *The Gendered Object*, Manchester, UK: Manchester University Press.

Klein, Naomi (2009), *No Logo*, 10th Anniversary Edition, Toronto: Vintage Canada.

Kotler, Philip and Kevin Lane Keller (2014), *Marketing Management,* 14th edition, Englewood Cliffs, NJ: Prentice Hall.

Krass, Peter (2004), *Blood and Whiskey: The Life and Times of Jack Daniel*, Hoboken, NJ: John Wiley.

Lee, Jerry (editor), (2013), *Gun Digest*, Blue Ash, OH: F+W Media.

Leffingwell, Randy (1995), *Harley-Davidson: History & Mystique*, Ann Arbor, MI: Borders.

Leffingwell, Randy (1996), Harley-Davidson: Myth and Mystique, Borders Press.

Leffingwell, Randy and Darwin Holstrom (2011), *The Harley-Davidson Motor Company: Archive Collection*, http://Www.motobooks.com/"ww.motobooks.com, London, UK: Motorbooks-imprint of MBI Books.

Littlefield, John and Julie L. Ozanne (2011), "Socialization into Consumer Culture: Hunters Learning to be Men," *Consumption, Markets and Culture*, 14 (4), 333–360.

Marcot, Roy (2005), *The History of Remington Firearms*, Guilford, CT: The Lyons Press.

Marcus, Phillip (n.d.), *Call of Duty: Black Ops II*, Activision: Treyarch.

Mark, Margaret and Carol S. Pearson (2001), *The Hero and the Outlaw: Building Brands through the Power of Archetypes,* New York: McGraw Hill.

Martin, Vivian B. and Astrid Gynnild (2011), *Grounded Theory: The Philosophy, Method and Work of Barney Glaser*, Boca Raton, FL: Brown Walker Press.

McCracken, Grant D. (1988), *The Long Interview,* Thousand Oaks, CA: Sage Publications.

McCullough, Kevin (2008), *The Kind of Man Every Man Should Be*, Eugene, OR: Harvest House Publishers.

McKibben, Gordon (1998), *Cutting Edge: Gillette's Journey to Global Leadership*, Boston: Harvard Business School Press.

Mueller, Mike (2008), *Ford Pickup Trucks, Motorbooks*, Minneapolis, MN: MBI Publishing.

Nixon, S. (1996), *Hard Looks; Masculinities, Spectatorship & Contemporary Consumption*, London: Routledge.

Nixon, S. (1997), "Exhibiting Masculinity," in Stanley Hall (ed.), *Representation: Cultural Representations and Signifying Practices*, London: Sage, 291–336.

Peter Fonda, Dennis Hopper and Terry Southern (1968), Dialogue by actor Jack Nicholson in the film "Easy Rider". Released by Columbia Pictures.

Rao, Vithala R., Manoj K. Agarwal and Denise Dahlhoff (2004), "How Is Manifest Branding Strategy Related to the Intangible Value of a Corporation?" *Journal of Marketing*, 68 (4), 126–141.

Reeser, Todd W. (2010), *Masculinities in Theory*, Chichester, UK: Wiley Blackwell.

Rose, Bob and Jean Buchanan (2008), *Anheuser Busch the King's Reign*, St. Louis: St. Louis Post-Dispatch.

Schouten, John and James McAlexander (1995), "Subcultures of Consumption: An Ethnography of the New Bikers," *Journal of Consumer Research*, 22 (June), 43–61.

Schroeder, Jonathan and Miriam Salzer-Morling (2005), *Brand Culture*, London: Routledge.

Schroeder, Jonathan E. and Detlev Zwick (2004), "Mirrors of Masculinity: Representation and Identity in Advertising Images," *Consumption, Markets and Culture*, 7 (1), 21–52.

Souter, Gerry (2012), *American Shooter: a Personal History of Gun Culture in the United States,* Dulles, VA: Potomac Books Inc.

Sparke, Penny (1995), *As Long as It's Pink: The Sexual Politics of Taste*, London: Pandora.

Thompson, Craig J., Aric Rindfleisch and Zeynep Arsel (2006), "Emotional Branding and the Strategic Value of the Doppelgänger Brand Image," *Journal of Marketing*, 70 (1), 50–64.

Thompson, Craig and Kelly Tian (2008), "Reconstructing the South: How Commercial Myths Compete for Identity Value through the Ideological Shaping of Popular Memories and Countermemories," *Journal of Consumer Research*, 34 (5), 595–613.

Thompson, Hunter S. (1967), *Hell's Angels: A Strange and Terrible Saga*. New York: Random House.

Thornton, Andrew D. (1993), "The Accomplishment of Masculinities: Men and Sports," in Tony Haddad (ed.), *Men and Masculinities: A Critical Anthology,* Toronto: Canadian Scholars' Press, 121–161.

Twitchell, James (2004), *Branded Nation: The Marketing of Megachurch, College Inc., and Museumworld*, New York: Simon and Schuster.

Twitchell, James (2006), *Where Men Hide*, New York: Columbia University Press.

United States Bureau of the Census (2010), *Census Population Estimates,* Census.gov.

Watson, Elwood and Marc E. Shaw (2011), *Performing American Masculinities*, Bloomington: Indiana University Press.

Watts, Trent (2008), *White Masculinities in the Recent South*, Baton Rouge: Louisiana State University.

Whitehead, S. M. (2002), *Men and Masculinities*, Cambridge: Polity Press.

Whitehead, S. M. and F. J. Barrett (2001), *The Masculinities Reader*, Cambridge: Polity Press.

Wolfe, Tom (1968), *The Electric Kool-Aid Acid Test*. New York: Farrar, Straus and Giroux.

Zahavi, A. (1975), "Mate Selection—a Selection for a Handicap," *Journal of Theoretical Biology*, 53, 205–214.

Zehr, Howard (2013), *Pickups: A Love Story,* Intercourse, PA: Good Books.

ZZ Top, album *Eliminator* (1983), Released by Warner Brothers Records, Written by Billy Gibbons, Dusty Hill, Frank Beard.

Index

Page numbers in *italics* refer to figures and tables.

Printed in the United States
by Baker & Taylor Publisher Services